The Inventor's Daughter

a memoir

Bonnie Greene LeVar

The Inventor's Daughter
A Memoir

Copyright ©2023 Bonnie Greene LeVar

ISBN   979-8-218-17757-7   Soft
ISBN   979-8-218-17756-0   Hard
ISBN   979-8-218-17758-4   eBook

Library of Congress Control Number 2023905714

Book design by Nan Barnes, StoriesToTellBooks.com

The Inventor's Daughter

a memoir

Bonnie Greene LeVar

Contents

Why Memoir?

"I believe the answer goes to the gigantic question of why people create art. And I believe it's because there is a need—an urgency, even—to express the truth: to take it from inside of us, from our personal, private experience, and place it outside of us, in whatever form we choose, using whatever tools we have. Then, there is—or can be—recognition and identification, revelation, comfort—human connection, really. What is more important?"

~Susan Hodara, author and teacher

Dedicated to my family—

past, present, and future—my grandchildren,

Sarah, Matthew, Charlotte, and Samantha.

CHAPTER ONE

My Father—"Fooled 'em again!"

My father teased us that he came from "good stock." That became a joke between my siblings and me when I changed it to "good soup!" Sometimes, we would go so far as to say that he came from "good chicken soup."

"Oh, my God!" I thought. "This can't be happening!"

We were at 35,000 feet, and there was my father – our pilot! —unconscious.

When the control tower in Washington, DC, advised him to watch out for a plane at our altitude carrying France's President Mitterrand, I scanned the clear blue air and saw it in the distance. I continued watching for other aircraft that might be around, and when I turned back toward my father, I saw his head slumped onto his chest, his eyes closed.

Did he have a heart attack? Was he dead? I didn't know whether to wake him or tell my husband, John, that we were about to die or attempt to figure out how to use the radio and have someone on the ground tell me how to land a plane the way I'd seen in action movies. My one relief was that I knew Dad had set the automatic pilot.

It was always a treat for my siblings to sit in the co-pilot seat of my father's plane, and my delight was no exception when it was my turn. I was thrilled to have one-on-one time with my father. I liked to read him the pre-flight checklist and have him answer "Check" after each step: "Clear right," "Check." "Clear left," "Check." "De-icing on," "Check," until the list was completed. If one of us inadvertently skipped a step, Dad knew immediately and let us know what we'd forgotten.

This time, though, I wasn't happy about playing co-pilot. My husband, John, and our two teenage children were flying home from a week in Florida. John sat in the cabin of the King Air reading while Jonathan and Joanie were sleeping comfortably. I was next to my father in the co-pilot seat, staring at him, willing him to wake up. It may have been just a minute, but it felt like a lifetime, and it took a massive effort on my part not to lose control—at least until I could figure out what, if anything, I should or could do.

Then, he lifted his head slowly, and I could breathe again. He reached around the back of his seat, pulled out an oxygen mask, and placed it over his nose. He took a deep breath, returned the inhaler, and looked at me with his powder-blue eyes. It would be a rough landing, he told me casually, and he had wanted a short nap to be "refreshed." I said nothing.

The airport came into sight. As we descended, it started snowing, and intense winds buffeted us in all directions. Finally, we taxied to a stop at the hangar. That's when Dad came out with one of his favorite quips: "Fooled 'em again!"

My father with a model of the King Air.

Leonard Michael Greene was born on June 8, 1918. His mother claimed she gave birth in the hospital elevator on her way up to the delivery room. Nobody knows if that is true, but it might explain my father's lifelong love of flying. It made a delightful story, and my father had many of them. Not the least of which was his family's history.

According to my grandmother's diary, her mother, Fanny Isaacs, my great-grandmother, lived and worked as a dress designer in Odessa, Russia. The story goes that the Czarina had seen Fanny's creations and wanted Fanny to design her clothes. So, she was invited to the Palace of Czar Alexander II to be interviewed by the Czarina. Fanny became the Czarina's head designer and was permitted to visit the palace whenever needed. She frequented a department store in Warsaw, Poland, to buy materials for her dresses, and on one of those trips, she met the store's owner, Jacob Furman, my great-grandfather.

(In the 1980s, the Metropolitan Museum of Art had an exhibition of Russian dresses from the Imperial Palace. My father went because he said his grandmother might have made one of them.)

A revolution broke out in Russia not long after my great-grandparents, Jacob and Fanny, were married. Many Jews were tortured and murdered. Gentile friends hid my great-grandparents in a cellar and helped them sneak across the border. They came to America in 1881, with thousands of other Jews escaping the pogroms. They gave birth to a baby girl who would become my grandmother on my father's side. They named her Lena, but everyone called her "Lyn." My grandmother's diary continues, "Dad (Jacob) started with his very meager pennies to sell trinkets in a pushcart in the streets [of New York]."

My other great-grandfather Louis Greenblatt came from a small town in Poland, where he was a Yeshiva student. He married Sarah, who was from a family of weavers. They arrived in America in 1880, and Louis quickly learned English. He became wealthy from the carriage robes and shawls he manufactured and sold to affluent customers. To avoid anti-Semitism, Louis legally changed their name from Greenblatt (meaning "Greenleaf") to Greene. They had a son, Maxwell (Max), my grandfather.

I don't know how they met, but Lena and Max married and had three children, one of whom was my father. When Dad was

16, Max died of stomach poisoning while traveling by boat to Cuba for business. Suddenly fatherless, the family and millions of others suffered the deprivations of the Great Depression. My grandmother Lyn told me they had only two eggs a week, and Dad got one because he was the youngest.

As a young man, Dad drove a taxi in New York City and eventually saved enough money to take flying lessons. He told me some terrifying stories about flying under bridges and other (stupid) tricks. Lucky for him (and me), he quickly overcame that phase. Perhaps the most significant experience in my father's life was witnessing a fatal airplane crash in 1937 when he was only nineteen. He watched, horrified, as a plane nose-dived into the ground. Not satisfied with accepting the accident as inevitable, Dad was determined to figure out what had gone wrong. And he did.

He constructed a lift detector, a small toggle switch applied to the wing, which would send a warning alarm to the pilot if the plane was about to stall. This invention, the Stall Warning Indicator, made my father famous. It led to his founding of Safe Flight Instrument Corporation in 1946 and the hundreds more patents issued to him during his life. He never bragged about it, but a Saturday Evening Post article published in 1947 said of his innovation, "It may be the greatest lifesaver since the invention of the parachute."

My mother

My Mother—What's Wrong?

My mother is lying on the grass, holding me up in the air like an airplane. We are laughing.

That is my first memory of her. I didn't know the pain that was to follow such joy.

The rest of my early memories of her are unhappy ones. When she was home, my mother spent her days in her bedroom with the door closed, and we were told not to bother her because she had a "headache." A housekeeper took care of my brother, Randy, my baby sister, Laurie, and me. This headache situation lasted for as long as I remember my mother living at home. I couldn't understand why she didn't want to see us.

My mother was different when she and my father went out at night. She was beautiful. I had seen pictures of movie stars, and she looked like one, with gorgeous dresses and matching hats with short veils that almost covered her brown eyes. If they had been violet, she would have looked like Elizabeth Taylor, with her fair skin and black hair. When she wasn't home, I'd rifle through her dressing room, uncap her Fire and Ice lipstick, and smell her Shalimar perfume in its bottle shaped like a seashell.

I don't have the same lifetime of memories with my mother as with my father. There are few photos and no diaries to connect me with her past. There are no stories similar to those of the Greenblatt's – of the lower East Side, the pushcarts, and poverty. I knew about my mother from infrequent meetings with her over the years and bits and pieces of information her relatives reluctantly divulged.

Beverly Ann Kaufman, my biological mother and daughter of Albert and Betty Kaufman (my grandparents), had two brothers (Larry and Bobby). My mother and uncles were born in New York and grew up in Mt. Vernon. I have no idea where the Kaufman family came from or when they entered the United States.

My mother lived in our house until I was five, when my father explained that she was sick and needed to go to a hospital. The only sickness I was aware of was her headaches, and I was confused about her upcoming hospital stay. My father didn't say how long she would be there, and I guess he probably wouldn't have known if I had asked.

My mother never returned home.

My father did not disparage her for the remainder of his life.

After her death at age 84, I tried to get more information about her family from Uncle Bobby, but he didn't disclose much. His lack of knowledge and curiosity about his heritage was apparent, and I felt I was intruding as if it were none of my business.

Frustrated, I searched the Internet and discovered the following obituary in the Boston Herald from 2009. I gleaned much of what I learned about my biological mother from her obituary.

"Beverly Anne Fox, 84, a resident of Chestnut Hill, passed away October 11th. She was a graduate of Fieldstone and Pine Manor College."

Suddenly I remembered my grandmother telling me that my mother had wanted to go to Russell Sage College, but instead, and against my grandparents' wishes, she married my father when she was seventeen.

The obituary went on*: "*

Known by intimates as Billie, she loved dogs, especially her dachshunds, riding horses, sailing and tennis as well as playing the trumpet, piano, and later in life the French horn and recorder."

I met Doris at a bridge club where I played weekly. She was astonished when she found out I was Leonard Greene's daughter. The first thing she said to me was that my mother used to be called "Billie." I knew that – Randy, Laurie, and I sometimes called her Billie, but never to her face. I wondered why Doris felt she had to tell me this. Did she guess that I didn't know much of anything about my mother?

Doris explained that her older sister went to high school with my mother and that her sister and my mother were such good friends that her sister was one of my mother's bridesmaids. I felt embarrassed that I knew nothing about my parent's wedding, nor had I seen any of their wedding pictures. Once again, I felt left out of my family's story.

Doris's family and my grandparents lived in the same Mt. Vernon neighborhood. I remember my grandparents' fieldstone Tudor as being grand, and I liked it when my father dropped Randy, Laurie, and me off at their house to visit them when we were pretty young. Grandpa Al gave me big hugs, and Grandma Betty sat on the couch, sang to me, and let me play with her pretty things. Randy went bear hunting in their backyard, which must have seemed more believable to him than the wilds of our Scarsdale yard! I don't remember Laurie at those visits; maybe she was too young.

As for my mother's love of music, sometimes at night, I'd hear her playing the piano when I was upstairs in bed. Years later, I recognized the piece she had played was "Fur Elise." I taught myself the beginning of the composition and used to try and play it as she did.

The obituary continued:

"A voracious reader and creative writer, she kept journals, wrote autobiographical reminiscences, and penned stories throughout her life."

When I was an adult with my own children, my uncle Larry's wife, Aunt Joan, told me that my mother had enrolled in a writing workshop at Bennington College in Vermont. One of her pieces was published in the school newspaper, and my mother was so proud that she sent a copy to me, Randy, and Laurie. She wrote, "Now that I'm a grandmother, and all my children are grown and leading their own lives, I can pursue a college degree."

All I could think of was the lie that her words represented. Did she honestly believe her statement, or was she embarrassed to write the truth of her life? Did she not realize that she had not been present physically or emotionally when we were growing up?

Her obituary concluded:

"Billie is survived by her brother Robert, three children of her first marriage, Randall, Bonnie, and Laurie, five grandchildren, and two great-grandchildren."

Even in death, the myth continued about her status as a mother, grandmother, and great-grandmother to the grandchildren she didn't know and the great-grandchildren she had never met. I felt the urge to correct the obituary, but I didn't.

My mother with Randy and me

CHAPTER TWO

Motherless in Scarsdale

"Let me out!" I scream repeatedly, but the woman ignores me and won't unlock my bedroom door. Looking around, I think of another way to escape my punishment. I climb up onto the window seat, open the window, and crawl gingerly onto the steep slate roof. Glancing down, I see the swimming pool far below. I want to go to Randy's room, but his window is blocked by a ridge in the roof. If I fall, will I land in the pool or on the ground? I'm so scared, but I can't go back because there's not enough room on the ledge for me to turn around. Shutting my eyes and pretending that I'm on the floor so I won't think about falling, I clutch the flat stones and lean in as close to the roof as I can. Slowly, I inch my way around the ridge until my fingers reach a small sill. I open my eyes and see Randy's window. He's sitting on his bed and doesn't notice me until I startle him as I bang on the glass.

18 Butler Road - Up on the Roof!

The first house I remember living in when my parents were still married was a large fieldstone Tudor on Butler Road in Scarsdale. When I escaped from my bedroom, I was four years old; my brother, Randy, was six, and we had a one-year-old sister, Laurie. Although we stayed in the house only a few years, I can picture it clearly—partly from memory and partly because I choose to drive past it whenever I am in the neighborhood. It's still hard for me to believe that I survived crawling across that treacherous roof.

The house, set back from the road, was surrounded by mature plantings and a flagstone patio that surrounded a kidney-shaped swimming pool. The bushes closest to the driveway had pink and white flowers with sticky petals that I liked to touch, trying to get as many as I could to stay on my fingers at once.

When my father and mother went on a two-week European vacation, they asked my Grandma Lyn to watch us while they were away. I don't know how long my grandmother lasted as our babysitter, but she soon hired someone to take over and returned to her apartment in Manhattan. Randy and I must have done something to cause the sitter to punish us by locking us in our bedrooms, and I was frightened of being locked in alone. When the sitter came upstairs and found my room empty and Randy and I playing in his room, she contacted our parents, who came back immediately. I was happy they were home, and the mean babysitter was gone, but nothing changed: My mother spent most of her time alone in her bedroom. I was quite a lonely child.

I was also scared of dogs: I would tremble and cry whenever one came near me. I was just two when my parents decided to get a dog. To cure me of my fear, Dad said I shouldn't cry because I would frighten the dog and make it cry.

My father loved to tell the story of how he cured me of my fear of dogs. He took the family to Atlantic City, where we walked on the boardwalk. A huge German Shepard approached us and, before my father could stop me, I walked right up to the dog, put my face against his muzzle, and said, "Don't cry, doggie!"

Confident that I had overcome my fear, my parents bought an English Cocker Spaniel. We named him Don't Cry, and I have loved dogs ever since. Don't Cry was a handsome back-and-white champion who won many ribbons at Madison Square Garden under his formal name, Skyridge Warrior. Whenever the subject of his nickname came up, Dad told people about my part in naming him.

When I was an adult, my Aunt Joan shared that my father had hoped their aborted European vacation might cure my mother's headaches, but it didn't. His next idea was to reduce her stress by moving the family to a smaller house. So, he bought one less than a mile away, on Whig Road.

Left to right Laurie, Randy, and Bonnie with 'Don't Cry'

12 Whig Road—Life with Father

The flagpole was the first thing I noticed about our new home on Whig Road. The house was a split-level ranch, with a slate path leading to the front door and a short driveway bordered on one side by colorful tulips and daffodils. The yard was small. It seemed dwarfed by the flagpole, which looked out of place with no flag flying.

Despite the move to a smaller house, my mother's "headaches" didn't go away, and she continued to spend a lot of time in her bedroom. I would tiptoe up to the second floor and peer down to the end of the pale blue carpeted hallway to see if her door was open. It usually wasn't, but I was allowed to go in when it was. There I'd find my mother lying fully dressed on top of the covers, curtains drawn to block out the light. I would walk quietly to stand by her side, hoping she would reach out her arms for a hug, but she never did. When I asked her if she felt better, she'd look at me blankly without saying a word. Not knowing what else to do, I left the room. Maybe, I thought, she would be different the next time. She never was, though, and eventually, I stopped trying. I was only five years old, but I knew something was wrong.

My mother with 'Don't Cry' and 'Madame' and their puppies

The cook and chauffeur who had lived with us on Butler Road were replaced by Elizabeth, who cooked and took care of Randy, Laurie, and me. I was disappointed that my mother didn't spend time with me, but I was even more upset when my father told me that she had to "go to the hospital to get better."

I was afraid. I cried as he held me on his lap. "What's wrong with her?" I asked.

He hesitated a moment and said, "Mommy had a nervous breakdown."

That didn't make it any easier for me. What was a nervous breakdown? All I knew was that my mother never looked sick.

High Point

I think I would remember the day my mother left for the hospital if she had said goodbye. But I don't, so she probably didn't. Maybe I thought she would be back soon because I was in the hospital for only a few days when I had an eye operation. I might have thought it would be like that for her. How was I to know that she would never come home again?

After a few weeks, my father took Randy and me to the hospital to visit our mother. (Laurie was too young to come with us). The drive seemed to take forever, but now I know that High Point Hospital was in Port Chester, on the Greenwich border -a half-hour from Whig Road. As we approached, the hospital appeared high on a hill behind a fieldstone wall and looked no different from the private homes in the neighborhood. It was a large stone mansion – more like our house on Butler Road than a hospital.

Inside, someone led us to a small waiting room. I expected to go to my mother's room and find her in pajamas in bed. However, I never saw her room or any other part of the hospital. Instead, she joined us in a room with a couch and a few chairs – dressed in good clothes and high heels. We sat there looking at one another with little talk, no games, and nothing to do. What kind of hospital was this? In my memories, my father wasn't with us. I was uncomfortable and wished I were back at home. But I also didn't want to leave my mother. After a while, it would be time for us to go—the moment I always dreaded.

We continued these hospital visits, although less and less frequently. Each one left me wanting more: more affection, more conversation, and more time with my mother. I remember those long, sad, silent afternoons watching my beautiful mother sitting in a high-backed armchair. I asked her when she would come home, but I got no answer. I begged her to go back with us. Why didn't she say that she wanted to? Had we done something wrong?

My last memory of High Point is the day I burst out crying as we were leaving. I got into the car's back seat with Randy and turned to watch my mother standing at the front door as we drove down the long driveway. When she was out of sight, I buried my face in the white lace handkerchief she had given me for my tears, the scent of her Shalimar enveloping me.

Adventures with Dad

My father was my superhero. He was slightly over six feet tall, with light brown hair and twinkly blue eyes. When he returned home from work, I raced into his arms. When it stormed at night, I ran into his room and jumped under the covers so that he could protect me from the thunder and lightning. I was not afraid of anything when he was around.

If my father was out or came home late from work, we ate dinner with Elizabeth on a card table in the den while watching TV. She chose the programs, and I still remember the musical introduction to the "Perry Como Show" and Dinah Shore blowing a kiss after her ditty "See the USA in your Chevrolet – America's the greatest land of all!" We were allowed to watch "Disneyland," my favorite show on Sunday nights. We ate Campbell's Chicken Noodle Soup and tuna fish sandwiches on white bread. Nothing was as enjoyable as soup and sandwiches in front of the TV.

On weekends, Dad took charge of planning things for us to do. The still-flagless flagpole became the source of one of his inspirations when he decided to turn it into a maypole. He tied streamers to the top, and we danced as we wound them around and around the pole until we had covered it with brightly colored crisscrossed ribbons.

The house had a full basement with a black-and-white linoleum floor and plenty of room for puppies. Now, along with Don't Cry, we had a second English Cocker Spaniel, an elegant blue roan named Madame, whom Dad told me was Don't Cry's wife. Don't Cry and Madame spent their days in retirement from the dog show circuit, keeping the pedigree well stocked. It seemed we always had a box of puppies that our friends would come over to play with until my father gave each litter away. As for Don't Cry, he slept at the foot of my bed every night until he died at age 16, during the same month I left home for my first year of college.

Laurie with an armful of new puppies!

Had my mother been home, would my father have been as resourceful about finding so many adventures for us to experience? He owned a plane that he used for testing his new inventions and for family trips. Larry and Caroline Hamilton were good friends of his, and they, along with their two children, became our traveling companions on many of our escapades. I looked forward to going places with their family because their children were our age, and Mrs. Hamilton was always happy to see me. She showed an interest in me. She treated me the way I wished my mother could. We walked with our arms around each other, and I liked to put mine around her slender waist.

Mrs. Hamilton's parents lived on a farm "far up north" (which might have been as close as Connecticut), and we drove to visit them one year to pick out a Christmas tree. (This is the time to say that my father did not raise us as observant Jews.) We rode through the forest in their horse-drawn hay wagon, searching for the perfect tree while marveling at the pristine snow and scent of fresh pine.

On another December day, Dad flew us to "Santa's Workshop." I have unsuccessfully tried to find out where this magical place was, but I can say that we left a snowless Scarsdale a short time later and landed in a very snowy "North Pole." Santa's workshop was a little village where elves bustled, helping Santa prepare for Christmas. I enjoyed trudging through the deep snow and watching all the pre-Christmas activities.

Although the house on Whig Road was not as large as the one on Butler, it had a flat backyard with enough room for a tennis court. Dad decided one winter to flood it and turn it into an ice rink for all the neighborhood kids. I didn't know how to skate, and when I told Dad I was afraid I'd fall, he handed me an aluminum chair and told me to push it around on the ice. He brought down extra chairs for any other new skaters. Clutching the blue-and-white webbed chair, I felt safe and quickly learned to skate. The rest of that winter, I practiced figure eights, spinning, and skating backward while dreaming of becoming a famous figure skater. I was also glad to make some new friends.

In the summer, Dad took us to the beach or sailing. He had a small boat that he sailed on the Long Island Sound. One sweltering day, he filled the cabin with buckets of water so Randy, Laurie, and I could splash around while he enjoyed being out on the Sound.

Another day we dropped anchor at a large rock somewhere in the Sound. Dad said it was "Treasure Island" and told us to search for the treasure that pirates had hidden there. I remember my delight as I picked my way around the tiny, treeless island and found lots of shiny new pennies scattered about by an unknown pirate.

Divorce

Despite our extravagant adventures, all I really wanted was for my mother to come home from the hospital. Instead, my father told me they were getting divorced when I was around eight. We weren't seeing her much, so I wasn't too surprised.

But I was sad. And I was confused. I often wondered about my mother's "nervous breakdown." My father explained it as best as he could, but to me, it was inexplicable. I never heard him criticize my mother or blame her for anything. It was a situation that I just had to accept.

It was unusual in the 1950s for a father to raise children as a single parent; no one else I knew lived with a father and no mother. I felt awkward around other children in the neighborhood and at school, and the other mothers didn't call to arrange play dates for me. Other families had mothers. My family was different, and I was plagued with embarrassment and guilt about it.

My mother moved to Stockbridge, Massachusetts, and became a patient at Austin Riggs Hospital; my father got custody of the three of us. After the divorce, Grandma Betty told me she would not come to our house anymore because she didn't want to be "disloyal" to my mother. That didn't make sense. I said I hadn't done anything wrong and she shouldn't punish me for my parent's divorce. As a compromise, she agreed to meet me in our driveway but refused to come inside.

My father hired a governess to help take care of us. Affectionately known as "Miss B," Elaine Bonkowski was petite with short wavy blonde hair. She dressed in skirts and heels, and whenever we went out, she wore a hat with a long feather on the side. I was fascinated by her eyebrows, which she tweezed off and then penciled back where hers had once been. Miss B was nice, but I never felt emotionally drawn to her. She was just another person who took care of us.

Disneyland

When I was eight, my father had to go to California for business and didn't want to leave us at home for an extended period. So, he persuaded our teachers to give us our assignments and promised them we would do our homework while we accompanied him on his trip.

My father's company, Safe Flight Instrument Corporation, owned a larger plane, a DC-3, big enough to fly us nonstop. Onboard, Dad hung hammocks from the plane's ceiling, and I fell asleep in one in White Plains, swaying gently all the way to California.

Flying to Disneyland in the DC-3!

We stayed at the Beverly Hills Hotel and visited a new amusement park called Disneyland. Its parking lot was bordered on both sides by glistening green grass, and it had a long, wide brick path leading to the park's entrance. We seemed to be walking forever, and I could hardly wait as other families joined us, all talking excitedly about our destination. When we got there, I saw the largest clock I had ever seen, perched on a grassy hill encircled by flowers of every color. I remember thinking it was a funny place to put a clock.

Inside the park, everything was clean and shiny. Food stalls and exhibitions surrounded a central plaza. My favorite cartoon characters—Goofy, Snow White, Mickey Mouse, and Donald Duck—strolled through the crowds, greeting visitors and offering handshakes and hugs. Some children were afraid to talk to them, but I wanted to meet them all.

My father handed us tickets to "Peter Pan's Never Land." I stood in line with Randy and hoped the ride wouldn't be scary. I grabbed his hand for protection as we entered a dark tunnel and climbed into a small pirate ship for two, attached to the pirate ship in front, like Randy's train set at home. Ours began to move, and we left the tunnel and headed into a new world. We flew out of Peter Pan's window on our way to Never Land. Beneath London Bridge, the city of London sparkled at night. The stars in the black sky twinkled like diamonds. It was the most beautiful place I had ever seen.

Sailing through the sky, London slowly disappeared, and an island in the distance got closer and closer. Our ship swooped down over Never Land, a desert island with pirates, Indians, and palm trees. Soaring above it, I never wanted our trip to end, but before long, the ship entered another dark tunnel, and we landed in sunny Disneyland, back where we had started.

Decades later, the first time I drove to Boston on I-84, I nearly went off the road when I approached Waterbury, CT. Going over a high bridge, I glanced down and saw a red brick watchtower standing tall over factories and tiny wooden houses. It brought me right back to Disneyland. Every time I drive past Waterbury, I remember my delight in flying to Never Land with Randy.

There were other trips and more fantastic exploits with Dad, but I could never forget that I didn't have a mother until I met Phyllis.

Grapefruit Trees in the Backyard

Because of my mother's hospitalization and my parent's subsequent divorce, I didn't get to spend much time with my mother's relatives. Still, I loved being with my Grandpa Al and Grandma Betty. Whenever I saw him, my grandfather would greet me with a warm bear hug and welcome smile. Grandpa Al was a short, stocky man with a large bald spot in the center of his head, surrounded by a semi-circle of gray hair. Grandma Betty was petite and unnaturally blonde. I thought she dressed stylishly and had beautiful jewelry, which I liked to try on.

They had a winter home in Palm Beach, Florida, and Randy, Laurie, and I once visited them when I was five. In their backyard stood two grapefruit trees, and I was allowed to choose my own for breakfast each morning. That was a special treat—picking real food from a tree! They had miniature cereal boxes; we could select whatever kind we wanted, open the box carefully, and pour the milk right into it.

Near the grapefruit trees was a swimming pool. It looked like the one we had at home—which I learned was called "kidney-shaped." We spent our days swimming and playing in the yard.

One night they took us to dinner at what must have been their club. We sat outside and ate at tables covered with white linen. The other diners were dressed in beautiful clothes, and the women wore lots of jewelry. I couldn't stop staring at all the sparkling diamonds and gold. Grandma Betty told me I had left our table and asked the "ladies" if I could see their "pretty jewelry." She chuckled as she told me that dinner was the origin of her nickname for me: "Diamond Lil."

On another night, we went to a hotel for dinner. The restaurant must have been on an upper floor because, when it was time to leave, Randy and I rushed to the elevator to go down to the lobby. Being seven, Randy was confident that he could take us by himself. Midway, the elevator stopped suddenly. I panicked as Randy pushed the buttons, trying to make it start back up. The lights stayed on, but I was terrified. I began to scream, "We're going to die! "We're going to die!" until the elevator started to move again, and we arrived safely at the ground floor. The door opened to a crowd of people, and when I ran out of the elevator, many were laughing. I spotted our grandparents, not laughing, waiting for us, and I tried to hide behind them. I didn't ride in an elevator again for years.

Grandma Betty and Grandpa Al in Florida

My First Funeral

When I was ten, I returned from school and found Randy sitting on our father's lap, crying. Randy never cried, and he didn't look like he had been hurt, so I was confused. My father told me that Grandpa Al had died. That's all I remember of that conversation. I got the details of his death more than 20 years later.

The next day, my father drove Randy and me into Manhattan and dropped us off at a huge building. He told us he would pick us up when it was over. What "it" was, I found out, was my grandfather's funeral. There was a large room filled with people, and we were ushered into the front row.

My mother grabbed Randy and me and dragged us to a small room at the back of the hall. She had her arm around my waist, and I could feel her shaking.

"You have to say goodbye to your grandfather," she said.

I didn't understand. We entered the room, and there he was—in an open casket. A dead person. My grandfather.

"Kiss him goodbye," she said.

"No," I screamed, backing away from the casket.

"Kiss him goodbye," she repeated, and I closed my eyes and tried to get out of her grasp. I felt his cold face, then ran out and back to the big room, where I saw Grandma Betty walking up the aisle. When she got to the front row, she wailed, began to faint, and was caught by someone near her. They brought out a wheel-chair, and she sat in it for the rest of the service.

As soon as I could, I left and was more than relieved to see my father standing by the entryway waiting for us. I threw myself into his arms but was too stunned to tell him what had happened. I couldn't wait to get out of there and go home.

I remember driving past city buildings, watching intently until I began to see trees and other signs of the country. As we crossed the bridge and, finally, pulled into our driveway, I silently con-gratulated myself for making it through the day without – what? I don't know. I only remember that I was overcome with relief. I silently swore to never go to New York City again.

After that, I got stomachaches each time we drove to the city. I felt as if I were going to throw up. I did not understand what frightened me, but I was scared. Randy, Laurie, and I, all under age 12, would sit in the car, and whether anyone spoke or not, I spent the entire ride staring out the window, watching the city come closer. I never told anyone how I felt because I was ashamed. It wasn't a feeling I understood. It was pure dread, and it took years before I understood that it was connected to my grandfa-ther's funeral.

Grandma Lyn

Unlike Grandpa Al and Grandma Betty, we saw my father's mother often. Dad drove Randy, Laurie, and me to visit Grandma Lyn in the huge pre-war apartment on Central Park

West that she shared with my Aunt Vic. Grandma Lyn was an artist and had hundreds of oil paintings stored in her home. In the living room, the couch was always covered in clear plastic. When we arrived, she would walk around the dim room plugging in lamps. I asked her about it, and she told me it saved money on electricity.

Grandma Lyn never got over the horrors of the Depression and spent the rest of her life spending money conservatively. She was the only woman in our family who cooked; everyone else had cooks and housekeepers. And she cooked like a Jewish grandma: lots of foods I hadn't eaten before, like brisket and latkes. She never made only one vegetable or dessert and encouraged us to eat everything. As a young child, I had no idea what "V for Victory" meant, but we held up our fingers in a "V" at every meal.

Despite her frugality, she and Aunt Vic went on cruises around the world. Grandma Lyn boasted that they always won the costume contests held on the ships. I liked to look through her photo albums at the extravagant hats my grandmother made for those contests. They were enormous, fashioned out of whatever they could find on the boat – paper doilies, straws, construction paper, and, sometimes, fruit.

Aunt Vic and Grandma Lyn enter a 'Hat Contest' on a cruise

But her most proud accomplishment, she told me, was that she started the Grandmother's Club of America. Being a grandmother was the only requirement for membership, so she invited Eleanor Roosevelt to join! While Eleanor politely declined, the Grandmother's Club achieved remarkable accomplishments. Its principal focus was to train women to become obstetricians. This was, in part, intended to advance women's careers when few professional occupations were available to them. At the same time, this new fleet of providers was employed to ensure healthy childbirth in low-income neighborhoods served by chapters across the country.

MRS. FRANKLIN D. ROOSEVELT
202 FIFTY SIXTH STREET WEST
NEW YORK 19, N. Y.

October 6, 1952

Dear Mrs. Greene:

I very much appreciate your invitation to join your Grandmother Club of New York City. I am so busy, unfortunately, I could not take any active part or attend meetings so I feel you would not want such a useless member.

With many thanks and my regrets,

Very sincerely yours,

Eleanor Roosevelt

Letter from Eleanor Roosevelt to Grandma Lyn

Phyllis—Good News!

One afternoon, I came home from school to find my father and Phyllis sitting on the couch in the den, looking pretty happy. I was surprised: Phyllis sometimes came to our house, but she had never been there on a school day.

I was an observant 11-year-old who longed for a mother and admired everything about Phyllis. She was easy to talk to and friendly. I admired her petite figure, deep brown hair and eyes, perfect hands, and polished nails. Her four sons—Doug, then age 14, Chucky 12, Donny, 10, and Stevie, 6—were good-looking, with their mother's high cheekbones and curly brown hair.

When my father first brought Phyllis home to meet Randy, Laurie, and me, I wasn't sure why she was there, but I immediately liked her. At that time, we had our governess, Miss B. Dad had many good friends, and sometimes we went on outings with their families. I always had fun, but I secretly pretended that their mothers were also my mother. I didn't attach any special meaning to Phyllis's visits until, on this day, I noticed a pear-shaped diamond ring on her left hand. "Are you getting married?" I blurted out without taking a breath.

"Yes," said my father. He was laughing. I think he was impressed that I had beaten them to the punch with their announcement, but I always paid attention to diamonds. Not to mention what this one might mean.

And now I couldn't believe my good luck. I was going to have a new mother! And it was Phyllis. Plus, we'd have four new brothers. I hoped they were as excited about our future family as I was. I couldn't wait!

Phyllis

Phyllis J. Saks was born in New York City on May 20, 1920. Her mother, Elsa Kahn, came from a prominent family of furriers in Germany. Elsa (whom we called Gaga) was an excellent tennis player who once competed in a tournament with the King of Sweden. Gaga told me that, after their match, he gave her an inscribed Fabergé egg with a tiny clock inside. She treasured that memento and said she was heartbroken when it was stolen from her hotel room in Sweden.

Phyllis's grandfather, Isidor Saks, and his brother, Andrew, started a men's clothing store in Washington, DC, and later expanded it to become Saks Fifth Avenue in New York, where, for the rest of her life, Elsa would get a considerable discount on anything she purchased. Sometimes, when I visited Gaga, she would take me shopping there and buy me beautiful clothes.

Phyllis never bragged about herself; most of what I learned about her past was from other people. Gaga told me that Phyllis had been a shy child. She was given horseback lessons and became an expert rider. She entered a horse show at Madison Square Garden and won a blue ribbon for "good hands." A leather-bound book of photos in our house included a picture of Phyllis on horseback jumping over a hurdle. I used to take it out and proudly show it to my friends.

Phyllis married Charles (Chuck) Freeman and had four sons. Chuck (known to our family as "Daddy Chuck") worked in advertising and created the logo for the New York Yankees. His photos reveal a handsome man with dark hair and a chiseled chin. He died of lung cancer when he was forty-five, leaving Phyllis a young widow, her four boys all under the age of ten.

CHAPTER THREE

"Camelot"

"In short, there's simply not
A more congenial spot
For happily-ever-aftering than here
In Camelot."

~ *"Camelot" (Lerner & Lowe) 1960*

The New Family—275 North Bedford Road

Nothing could equal my excitement about having Phyllis become my new mother. She made me feel special and treated Randy, Laurie, and me the way a "real" mother would: a different experience for us. Dad didn't need to entertain us extravagantly or fly us somewhere to be occupied. We simply enjoyed being together. The icing on my happiness cake was the thought of Phyllis's sons becoming my brothers. I looked forward to being in a large family.

After Phyllis and our father announced their engagement, our two families got together on weekends at either our house or Phyllis's large red brick colonial in White Plains. Phyllis's sons were friendly and handsome, and I loved being in their company. Indoors or outside, whatever they were doing, they invited us to join. They had a full attic that had been converted into a playroom, and we spent hours playing games like Foosball and ping-pong up there. Across the street from their house was a golf course where we tobogganed in the winter.

In preparation for the wedding, Phyllis took Laurie and me shopping for our outfits. We chose matching white organza dresses with white satin sashes at our waists. Our hairbands were fashioned out of simple white flowers. Phyllis looked beautiful in a pale grey silk dress with random splashes of hand-painted lavender and blue flowers.

On June 8, 1958, my father's 40th birthday, the entire bridal party met in the Rabbi's study for pictures. The boys wore dark slacks and light blazers—except for six-year-old Stevie, who wore light blue Bermuda shorts and a matching jacket. Then the seven of us marched down the aisle of Temple Israel, in White Plains, as best men and bridesmaids to our respective new parents.

The Wedding Party! Back row: Dad, Phyllis, Doug, Front row: left to right Bonnie, Randy, Laurie, Chuck, Stevie, Donny

The wedding reception, held at Phyllis's sister Anne's house in Mamaroneck, involved more picture-taking of all the children getting in on the cake cutting—and tasting! The guests, mostly relatives from both families, were served a luncheon in the spacious backyard. What I remember most about that afternoon was the laughter and how happy everyone was.

Our new parents went to Italy for a short honeymoon before taking us to Canada while our future home was being renovated. It was set to be completed for our arrival in time to start the school year. Before our trip, we piled into two station wagons and drove to the new house. To start our combined family with no home-court advantage, Dad and Phyllis had each sold their homes and bought a 200-year-old colonial set on seven acres in Chappaqua. We would all have our own bedrooms. We would all be attending new schools and making new friends. And we'd all be getting to know one another better.

At this point, none of us kids had ever heard of Chappaqua, and we weren't pleased about being in some strange town in the middle of nowhere. As we drove up Route 120 from White Plains, we stopped at a light at the bottom of the hill, where Bedford Road intersects with King Street. Straight ahead was the most decrepit house I had ever seen. It had faded white paint peeling off, and it looked like it was about to topple into the busy street. My stomach dropped, and I thought that maybe moving wasn't such a great idea. When the light was green, my father turned right and kept driving. *That's a relief, I* thought as he approached a stately house on beautiful grounds and parked the car.

"Countdown!"

Dad made our blended family official and adopted Phyllis's four sons. The adoption took place in Manhattan in a judge's chambers. The judge looked at us solemnly, and the seven of us took his cue and sat quietly as the proceeding took place. When he asked if we all approved, I held my breath, praying that no one would say "No." One by one, we each said, "Yes," and raced out of the room, cheering.

The celebration planned for the adoption included dinner at Trader Vic's and then "The Music Man," a new Broadway musical. We managed this by splitting us up again into the two station wagons. We sat in oversized rattan chairs at Trader Vic's, drank soda from coconut shells, and headed to the theater after dinner. Lining up for our tickets, someone noticed that Donny was missing! Dad rushed back to Trader Vic's and found him waiting calmly for us outside the bathroom. From that day on, whenever we went somewhere, Dad instituted "Countdown!" Doug, the oldest, was number one, then Randy, Chucky, me, Donny, Laurie, and Stevie. Dad or Phyllis (whom I soon called Mommy) would announce "Countdown," and we'd go in order, each of us, one at a time, starting with Doug shouting "one" and ending when Stevie called out "seven."

In April 1959, the family added the number "eight" when our sister Terry was born. Terry's birth was anticipated with much glee. We voted on whether we wanted a boy or a girl, and every night at dinner, we would lobby for the chance to pick the baby's name.

We formed two bowling leagues – the Banana Noses and the Gang Greene—and spent many rainy Saturdays bowling at Crossroads in Mt. Kisco. We'd ask Dad to take us to Carvel on hot summer nights. Loving games as he did, he told us he'd take us if we could get him there by giving him directions in the car. We took turns telling him to drive "straight," "left," or "right." The challenge was that Dad always got to choose the fourth turn, and he purposely turned in the wrong direction. We had to strategize our directions so that the final turn would land us at Carvel no matter what route he took. We always won. But I don't think Dad felt like a loser: He liked ice cream as much as we did! He explained his late-night raids to the kitchen for a bowl of ice cream as the only cure for his nocturnal sore throats.

The house came with a red barn and a chicken coop. I had seen the barn but did not know about the coop until my first night sleeping in my new bedroom. Around dawn, I heard a screeching noise that sounded like it was coming from under my bed. Terrified, afraid that whatever monster might attack me was hiding there, I stood on the bed and jumped to the doorway without touching the floor. Then I ran across the hall into my parents' room, waking them with my cries for help. My father ushered me back into my room, looked under the bed, and assured me nothing was there. Then the screeching began again. "It's a rooster," my father said, laughing. "He's in our backyard." He said that it seemed so close because my window was open. I don't recall ever seeing or hearing a rooster again.

Fire

The third floor was where my brothers decided to make fire-bombs out of rubber cement. My father's family had been in the rubber cement business, so we had gallons of the stuff around the house. I liked to take some and roll it around in my hands to make little balls—sort of like Silly Putty. One day the boys thought it would be fun to light the rubber balls on fire, toss them out of a window onto the driveway, and watch them explode. When that wasn't exciting enough, they put a bunch of fireballs into a large plastic bag and threw it out Chucky's window. It hit the tree next to the house, and the tree caught fire. Somehow, they put out the fire—but that was the end of our access to rubber cement.

It was also the beginning of our fire safety lessons. My father got the fire department to send over a firefighter to lecture us about the dangers of fire and how to protect ourselves. First, we were shown a frightening movie. Then we were given instructions on how to escape our rooms: "drop, roll, and crawl" to the door; feel the door for heat. Each room was outfitted with a rope ladder that was attached under a windowsill. Stevie thought the rope was great fun and tried it out until he got into trouble for it. As for me, I swore there was not a chance I would ever go out my window and down a rope to the driveway. (I was a more adventurous four-year-old when I climbed out my window to get to Randy's room.)

Terry was a baby, and our parents wanted to make sure she was taken to safety in the event of a fire. Dad gave Doug the job of going into Terry's room and carrying her out to the driveway. One day the fire alarm went off. Forget the ladders. I ran to Terry's room, at the top of the stairs, and found everyone had had the same idea. Someone else had already "rescued" Terry, so I rushed down the stairs and "rescued" Mommy's fur coat in the hall closet next to the front door. I have been teased about this for years, but why let a perfectly good coat burn? The alarm went off a few more times until my father discovered that the cause was mice eating the wires in the basement.

Lillie

When Phyllis was a young mother to four sons, Lillie helped her with housekeeping and cooking. Lillie continued to help and comfort her during the years after Phyllis was widowed and caring for her family while, at the same time, pursuing a graduate degree as a guidance counselor.

The first time Randy, Laurie, and I slept over at Phyllis's house, Chucky told us about "the cake." After everyone had finished dinner and Lillie had cleaned the kitchen and gone to bed, we sneaked downstairs to find it. There it was—a three-layer chocolate cake—"hidden" in the pantry on a low shelf just within our sight. We helped ourselves to huge pieces and probably made a mess. The following day, nothing was said about any missing cake or chocolatey crumbs. This routine continued until Dad and

Phyllis married, and we all moved to the new house. Lillie came to live with us and quickly became a member of our newly expanded family. Unfortunately, the hidden cake routine did not move to Chappaqua with Lillie.

I was eleven when I first met Lillie and was fascinated by everything about her. A statuesque woman in her fifties, Lillie had salt-and-pepper hair styled in a net-encased bun. Her soft brown eyes could turn sharp when one of us licked the mixing bowl before she was finished with it or if we were squabbling with one another in the kitchen.

Lillie wore a uniform: a light gray dress with a white Peter Pan collar and a starched white apron on top. She crisscrossed the straps of the apron and pinned them in the back with a straight pin. I wondered why the pin didn't come out—and why she didn't use a safety pin. I never asked her, however. It was part of her mystique. Looking back, it occurs to me that she didn't need that apron: it was never stained.

We all loved Lillie. At one time or another, we each laid our heads on her ample bosom and felt the comfort of her arms around us as we cried over one thing or another. For me, Lillie was there, every day as someone who listened to my stories, told me about her life, or chatted with me while I sat at the long wooden table and watched her bake or cook dinner.

Whatever Lillie prepared was delicious. She didn't use a cookbook, and whenever I asked her how to make something, she would answer "a little of this," "a handful of that," or "cook at medium temperature until done" (we had a large gas stove with no "medium" dial). I never saw her use a measuring cup, and I never saw her stressed about how anything would turn out. Sometimes she would surprise us with one of our favorite meals—roast beef —and our most prized dessert: chocolate steamed pudding with a butter sauce that melted the pudding on our plates.

Seven years later, when Mommy died, I rushed home from college. Lillie wasn't there; I learned she had left the day before. I had no chance for goodbyes. I never understood why she had left us so suddenly, and I never saw our beloved Lillie again.

"Worm"

We all had nicknames, and the youngest of my new brothers, Stevie, arrived in Chappaqua with his. He never stopped moving. Mommy told me that when he was a baby, they had to put a lid on his crib to keep him from climbing out. Stevie could worm his way into—and out of—anything. Hence the nickname "Worm."

The Chappaqua house had a two-stall stable with a riding rink along with a barn and chicken coop. My father bought a horse, Kentucky Girl, whom Stevie hopped right up on and had to be pried from whenever he was told to come in. Stevie didn't bother with a saddle; he just rode around, jumping the fences joyfully. The horse was a gift for Mommy, who had once been a champion rider, participating in horse shows in Madison Square Garden as a young woman. I don't remember seeing her ride Kentucky Girl more than a few times around the rink. She may have been too uncomfortable with ovarian cancer that none of us knew she had.

When Stevie wasn't outside, he found all sorts of things to keep himself occupied. He disassembled the stove—and then put it back together. Lillie was furious, but my father was impressed. Being five years older, I tried to boss Stevie around, but never very successfully. I once attempted to force him to do my bidding, but our wrestling match ended in a painful tie, and I didn't try that again. I thought it was funny, as did the other siblings who were watching.

"LEGS"

Laurie's nickname was "Legs," a double entendre of sorts: her initials were LEG, and she had very long legs. When I read Grandma Lyn's diary, I saw that she said she was called "Chicken Legs" because of her tall, skinny body when she was young. I guessed that Laurie must have looked like her.

I have a few memories of Laurie from the years before we moved to Chappaqua when she and I shared a bedroom. The earliest and most unpleasant is of her nightly screams. She insisted that she had terrible earaches, but I didn't believe her. For whatever reason, I thought she was faking. All I knew was that she woke me up crying every night and didn't stop until our father entered the room. I don't know what he did to calm her down; I wish I had asked him. Eventually, she had a tonsillectomy, and the night crying stopped.

It was then that I decided to torture Laurie. I would sneak into the closet after she was asleep and make noises, causing her to run out of the room, afraid of the ghost.

I wasn't always mean to my sister. Sometimes we would play with our dolls. We would take baths together, sing "Miss Lucy had a baby..." and giggle. We might have been closer if Dad hadn't married Phyllis. I couldn't control my happiness when we moved to our Chappaqua house, filled with a new mother, four new brothers, and, a year later, a baby girl. Laurie and Randy didn't appear to be as thrilled with the new family as I was.

If Laurie was displeased with something, only Doug could get her in a better mood, and he knew it. Whenever she got angry or upset, he would say, "I bet I can make you smile," and Laurie would say, "No, you can't!" Then Doug would wink at her, and no matter how hard she tried to resist, Laurie would look away, break into a smile, and laugh. These winking contests took place at the dinner table, witnessed by all of us, who would tease Laurie mercilessly. The rest of us would try to make Laurie laugh, but Doug was the only one who succeeded.

Laurie took Terry under her wing as Terry constantly tagged along behind her while Laurie sang her wild Western songs with hooting. They also held gentle tea parties hidden away from the rest of the family under our yard's thick boughs of spruce trees.

Donny

Donny was the nicest person I have ever met. He tended not to join his brothers' crazy antics, like their firebomb experiment. He and I were close because I wasn't exactly a daring person either. Donny was intelligent, studious, and liked to get along with everyone. For reasons I neither agree with nor understand, his nickname was "Bozo."

One winter, after a heavy snowfall, Donny wanted to shovel the neighbor's driveway to make spending money. The job took him all day to finish, and when he asked Dad what he should charge, Dad suggested that Donny tell the owner to pay him what he thought was fair. Donny followed that advice, and the owner paid him $5. That was the last time Donny did that!

Always coming up with ideas or problem-solving, Donny was much like Dad. Home to such a large family, our house could get pretty messy. And, as illustrated, one of us occasionally caused some sort of problem. Rather than setting up a list of chores for us to do or punishing us for some transgression, our father implemented a system of merits and demerits. He kept a small notebook and pencil in his pocket to keep track of each of our total scores. In response, we all went crazy, cleaning our rooms and closets and doing whatever we could think of to accumulate merits. When one of us got in trouble, Dad looked profoundly serious as he took out the book and issued the dreaded demerits. This system lasted for quite a while, until one night at dinner Donny asked Dad, "What is a merit worth?"

Finding Dad with no answer at the ready, we figured out we had been had! We had Donny to thank for dismantling the system, or we would have been cleaning the house for years.

Doug

Doug was good-looking, with dark brown hair, brown eyes, and straight white teeth. He also had a killer smile and a great sense of humor. I never understood why Chucky called him "Ears." It seemed like a stupid nickname, and I never cared enough to ask why. I did call Stevie "Worm," but I never called Doug "Ears."

Hard as it was for me to believe, Doug wasn't perfect. When angry about something, he'd stomp down the stairs from his room and crack his toes on each step. It amazed me that he could do that, but I stayed out of his way whenever I heard his toes cracking.

Because Doug was three years older than I and a freshman in high school, I didn't consider having a crush on him – or his cute friends. That fact probably saved me from making a fool of myself. However, I liked to "spy" on Doug and his friends and eavesdropped on them talking about the girls they liked. Doug and his friends hung out with the cheerleaders and the most popular girls in school. Because he was so grown up, I never imagined that one day Doug and I would become friends.

On the other hand, my girlfriends had no problem getting Doug to pay attention to them. On any given day, I had at least one friend who wanted to come to our house after school to hang out. Aside from the opportunity to be around Doug (if he were home), there was also Chucky, who was twelve. Chucky didn't mind the influx of girls at the house; eventually he went out with one of my good friends.

Randy

Randy was thirteen and from my "original" family, and I didn't pay much attention to him with so many new brothers to get to know. Unlike with Doug and Chucky, I couldn't imagine any girls wanting to go out with him. I was wrong. My best friend had a crush on Randy for years. Randy's nickname, like Laurie's, was from his initials: "RAG."

One year, during a family vacation in Key West, Randy and Doug announced that they had made dates for the night. I told them I thought they were lying. Doug insisted, but I said I didn't believe them. They were supposed to meet the girls in the parking lot in front of our motel and take a taxi somewhere. Laurie and I snuck out of the motel, hid behind a palm tree, and waited to see what would happen. Sure enough, two girls arrived, and Doug and Randy went out to meet them. As they got into the taxi, Doug stuck his head out of the window and spotted us behind the tree. He said, "I told you so!" with a wide grin as he looked at Laurie and me.

Not long after the trip to Key West, my brothers decided to make a trapeze from the barn roof to a tree across the riding rink. I don't remember who tried it out first (probably Stevie), but I remember when it was Doug's turn. I was petrified that the wire would break. I told Doug to give me his class ring because I feared it would hurt while he was hanging onto the bar. He threw it to me as I watched. Not two feet out, the wire snapped, and Doug fell and landed on his back. Stevie ran to the house to get Mommy, who came down to the barn and put a blanket over Doug while we all waited for the ambulance. Chucky jumped off the roof and started to pace back and forth beside Doug. "What can I do to help?" Chucky asked him. Without skipping a beat, Doug calmly answered, "You could get off my hand." Horrified, Chucky stepped off of the blanket, which was covering Doug's hand. Even in terrible pain, Doug never lost his sense of humor.

Doug spent the next month in bed with a damaged kidney and a broken arm.

Chucky

Affectionately known as "Chuckles," Chucky was only a year older than I when we met; he was in seventh grade, and I was in sixth. Chucky had a light sprinkling of freckles over his nose and cheeks, medium brown hair curling in all directions, and brown eyes: He reminded me of the Beaver! We became fast friends, both of us new to our school. Chucky was happy, easy to get along with, and never instigated dumb ideas like trapezing across the riding rink. He did, however, go along with all of them.

Chucky, Doug, and Randy lived on the third floor of our house. Chucky's room was directly above mine, and he would sometimes tap messages to me on his floor. In hindsight, I am not sure how I was supposed to decipher those messages since neither of us knew Morse code.

Chucky's closet was built into the side of his wall, adjacent to a small closet in the hall next to his room. There was a hole between his closet and the hall closet that no one had noticed. Normally, this would be insignificant information, but in our home, the room belonged to the owner of a pet boa constrictor. This long yellowish snake lived in the closet when it wasn't hanging around Chucky's neck. When it was out of the closet, I stayed as far as possible from them both. One day Chucky came home from school to find his beloved boa missing. The aforesaid hole in the closet had been its escape, and we were forced to search the entire house for the escapee. Eventually, it was found nesting in some bedclothes.

Terry

Terry, the "yours, mine, and ours" baby, was a constant source of entertainment. We all loved to play with her from the start.

Because of our 12-year age difference and my (preoccupied) status as a new teenager, I don't have any memories of specific remarkable events until we grew older and I returned from college. What I do recall from childhood is the fun we had with Terry. She followed us around—like a little puppy, I thought. That's how we treated her, tossing her around and making her laugh. Being the youngest, Terry's nickname was "Runt."

Terry, age two, dancing and keeping us smiling.

Dinnertime

A mahogany table and ten light blue leather chairs took up much of our dining room. That's where we ate most nights because the kitchen table wasn't very comfortable for seven children, plus a highchair and two adults. French doors on one side of the room led to the porch and backyard. On the other side, near the head of the table, two built-in corner cabinets displayed Mommy's most treasured possessions—eight antique Chinese teapots. I liked looking at them—each one was unique with different shapes and painted with flowers, birds, or both. Mommy never talked about the value of things, but I guessed they must have been quite old and valuable.

We didn't have assigned seats except for Terry, whose high-chair was always next to my father. He sat at one end of the table, Mommy at the other, giving them ample opportunity to watch us in action. As we passed platters around, no one wanted to be the last to get their food – their piece of fried chicken, or worse, the family favorite, chocolate steamed pudding. We called that seat "Starvation Corner," and since we didn't know which seat would be the first to pass the platter, we never knew who would end up sitting there. I tried to place myself in what I hoped would be the middle of the platter passing.

We each had glasses of milk with dinner, except for Dad, who drank buttermilk with his meal. Every once in a while, his glass would end up at the wrong seat, and whoever drank his buttermilk by mistake was sure to grimace and complain. I made that mistake once—and vowed never to taste buttermilk again. From then on, I would take a tiny sip from my glass to be sure that it was, indeed, milk. I couldn't understand why anyone would willingly drink buttermilk.

The only one who never had the buttermilk experience was Laurie. That was because she couldn't talk without gesturing dramatically, and she managed to knock over her glass at every meal, milk or buttermilk.

Terry sat in her high chair and was entertained by whatever was going on. She liked to try to chew turkey legs, which my father was delighted to give her. We called her Henry the Eighth when she tried to lift the heavy leg.

Chucky had the bad habit, according to Mommy, of leaning back on his chair. After telling him repeatedly not to do this, Mommy said we had permission to tip him over if he did it again. Which, of course, he did, and Doug tipped him over. Then ensued a competition of Chucky trying to tip Doug over and Doug trying to tip Chucky over, which always ended up with Mommy warning, "Careful - watch the teapots!"

Stevie was on the school wrestling team and decided he would have a better advantage if he qualified for a lighter weight category. Despite Mommy's pleas, he sat at the table and refused to eat. He pushed his food around on the plate and lost so much weight that his lips started to bleed. Chucky was also on the wrestling team and only ate celery all day and at dinner. That wasn't a problem as far as I was concerned because I got to eat his dessert. I thought that Chuck and Steve were ridiculous, but I wasn't too worried about their health because wrestling season was relatively short. But Dad was upset and wrote a letter to the school athletic department suggesting they impose a rule that no wrestler be allowed to lose more than five pounds.

Randy and Donny were taking flying lessons and liked talking to Dad about each new experience. Donny was so eager to become a pilot that he got his pilot's license before his driver's license. Sitting at dinner, they would often compare notes.

Sometimes our family dinners fueled heated discussions. We spent many nights debating whether or not to build a fallout shelter. We spoke of the threat of Russia dropping atomic bombs on America, so we discussed 1) did we want to live underground in a shelter? 2) what food would we stock up on? And 3) How long would we have to stay in the shelter? I remember the list included water, tuna fish, and peanut butter. I had just read "On the Beach" and was having nightmares about the end of the world. The discussion boiled down to "Do you want to live the rest of your life in a shelter? Or do you want to die with the rest of humanity? Although we never did agree on whether or not to build the shelter, my father never built one, so I guess he did decide.

Most nights, my father told us riddles. For example: How could three missionaries and three cannibals cross the river if they had one canoe that could carry no more than two people? Cannibals could not outnumber missionaries, or the missionaries would get eaten. There were endless possibilities, but we never got it right, no matter how many nights we worked this riddle. We had a great time trying to figure it out—and we must have proposed hundreds of solutions, but we eventually gave up once we finished dessert. I loved those meals -with my father encouraging us to play mind games. Even now, as an adult, I sometimes refer to an impossible situation, with no apparent solution, as the "missionaries and cannibals dilemma."

Thanksgivings were spent at our house, with grandparents, aunts, uncles, and cousins joining us for turkey dinner. We would go outside and play running bases in the sideyard, which flooded each time it rained. Christmas was also a time for all the relatives to come over. Although Jewish, we had a tree with many presents scattered around. I thought we had the perfect family. Finally, life was as it should be.

Our Family!

Camp Waziyatah

I stood with the other campers and their parents as a seaplane circled the grounds of our camp and landed on Long Pond, the camp's lake. I watched in astonishment as my father and Mommy Phyllis stepped onto the dock! It was visiting day, and I'd assumed they'd be driving up to see me. I was a little embarrassed by the fuss their arrival created, but I also thought it was pretty cool. Mostly, though, I was excited that they had come.

I was ten when my father put me on an evening train bound for Portland, Maine. It was a sleeper car reserved for girls from the New York area going to Camp Waziyatah. It would be my first summer at sleepaway camp, and I didn't know anyone else on the train. I rarely had sleepovers with friends and was nervous about being away from home for two months. I lay on my stomach in my bunk bed, which I had seen the porter pull down from the ceiling with a long narrow key, and looked out the dusty window, watching the scenery change from the suburbs to the rural countryside. We traveled through the night, the train whistling as we passed railroad crossings and other places I couldn't make out.

The rhythm of the tracks kept me company as I wondered if the camp would be as much fun as the people who had come to our house to show me pictures of Camp Waziyatah had promised it would be. And I also thought about what it might be like after camp was over, two months after my father and Phyllis were married when we would all move into a big house in Chappaqua. I couldn't wait. I couldn't believe I would soon have four new brothers! Beyond the train window, lights dotted the darkness in the distance. Before long, I fell asleep.

I don't remember who took me to Saks Fifth Avenue to shop for the required uniforms and other supplies in preparation for camp, but it was probably our governess, Miss B. The list included enough paraphernalia to fill a large metal trunk: white polo shirts, gray cotton shorts, gray woolen Bermuda shorts, and red sweaters with gray piping. Everything had to be labeled with my name – even my socks and underwear had nametapes. Saks did it all, including sewing on all the clothing. The next time I saw that trunk was when I got to camp.

We were also required to buy a particular woolen blanket. It was called an Indian blanket – off-white with thin red, green, and blue stripes. It was heavy, and I liked to bury myself in it during the cold Maine nights. I loved that blanket and slept with it on my bed at home for years.

In Portland the following morning, we were met by counselors waiting beside a bus that would take us to our final destination in Harrison, about a two-hour drive. The camp spread out over sweeping lawns, with Long Pond surrounded by pine trees. Dark brown wooden cabins were separated into two campuses—"The Pines" for the younger campers (me, obviously) and "The Hill" for the older girls. The most senior campers, age 13, lived in a large cabin overlooking the lake. It was called "The Ledge," and I vowed to stay a camper until I could live there.

The cabins had screens for windows and doors. Maine was freezing at night, so I slept in sweatpants and a sweatshirt, which I wore to breakfast every day. By the time breakfast was over, it had warmed up, and I changed into shorts or a bathing suit, depending on my schedule.

Before starting our activities, we made our bunk beds and spun the chore wheel on the wall to see our daily tasks. My favorite was sweeping the main room and bathroom because it was the easiest. Other jobs included holding the dustpan for the sweeper, taking out the garbage, removing the towels from the clothesline, and sweeping the porch.

I made friends with my bunkmates and reveled in feeling no different from the other girls. They didn't know that I had lived in a house without a mother, one who was a patient in a mental hospital. It was a relief not to be singled out or pitied.

Each night, as we entered the large dining hall, the owners, Leonard and Beatrice Fields, greeted us one by one as we held out our hands for inspection. No dirty nails or fingers allowed! I was terrified at the thought of being sent back to the cabin to rewash mine, so I can honestly say that my hands were never again as clean as they were that summer.

We had to write letters home once a week and turn them in as meal tickets when we arrived at the dining hall. I didn't mind; I wrote every week asking my father to send snacks and other contraband. (He didn't.)

On Friday nights, we had vespers. I had never heard of vespers but soon realized it was a non-denominational (yet Jewish style) service where we sang songs. It was peaceful, sitting on logs on a hill facing the lake at sunset.

We also had campfires where we sang songs that I still remember. There was one for every activity. Each summer, I sing the swimming song to my grandchildren whenever we go to the beach or pool:

> *"Swimming, swimming, in the swimming pool.*
> *When days are hot, when days are cool, in the swimming pool.*
> *Breaststroke, sidestroke,*
> *fancy diving, too.*
> *Don't you wish that you could have nothing else to do – but…*
> *swimming!"*

I especially enjoyed canoeing. We paddled on nearby lakes and camped overnight in tents. One summer, I used the outdoor facilities (a leaf instead of tissue paper) as needed. By the next day, back in camp, I had a widespread, itchy rash on my butt and had to be seen by the camp doctor. I was miserable and humiliated by having a male doctor examine my bare bottom. I was diagnosed with a bad case of poison oak. I never used the leaf trick again. On another three-day trip, when I was an older camper, we slept with our heads under our canoes. No tents – just our sleeping bags sticking out of the canoes. It poured for two days, and everyone and everything was soaked.

Being goal orientated, I worked hard to reach the highest swimming level, which would entitle me to special swim privileges. Green caps were for beginner swimmers, then red, white, and gold. By my second summer at camp, I had advanced to gold and was permitted to swim out to the raft and the deep water.

Long Pond was two miles long, and only the top swimmers were allowed to try to swim its length. During my last summer, I qualified, and a counselor and lifeguard rowed me to the other end of the lake early one morning. I entered the cold water, and they followed me in the rowboat as I swam. Now, as much as I liked swimming, I had an aversion to dead fish – specifically to touching one. Their bloated bodies and slimy eyes disgusted me. Most of the long-distance swimmers did the crawl, but I swam the entire lake using the breaststroke so I could spot any dead fish and swim around them. After what felt like an interminably long time, I reached my target: the beach at the end of the lake. The whole camp was waiting for me and cheering! They sang the song reserved for this accomplishment. I was a hero – an honor only a few campers attained yearly.

I loved Camp Waziyatah and returned every year until I was 13, old enough to live in "The Ledge."

And back in Chappaqua, when I started middle school, the first person I met was a girl from my first bunk at camp. We remain friends to this day.

"Los Rockets"

After I "aged out" of Camp Waziyatah, I went to summer school. As much as I missed the lake, the canoe trips, and the smell of the pines, I soon learned that summer school wasn't so bad.

The summer between 9th and 10th grades, my best friend, Betsy, and I enrolled in a Spanish immersion course at the Universidad Technologic de Monterrey, a small city in northern Mexico. We would be part of a group of Westchester students chaperoned by a local Spanish teacher, so we were allowed to go with our parents' blessings. And I'm pretty sure we got credit for the class.

We lived in a dorm with an outdoor pool—a necessity, I quickly discovered, because I had never been so hot in my life: no fans and no air conditioning, just the brutal heat. The minute I got out of class, I raced for the pool. I was sure you could fry an egg on the cement surrounding it, but I never got to test my theory because I failed to pocket an egg from the cafeteria.

When the afternoon cooled down a bit, Betsy and I would walk into town. Our school was on a hill, and we meandered down narrow streets to the center, where shops and small cafes existed. I browsed in the record shop, which sold albums from a local rock-and-roll band called Los Rockets. I had never heard of them but on their album cover they were dressed in white suits and looked like the Beatles.

One night we went to a club—more like a bar with a stage—and listened to Los Rockets. Even though we were underage in New York, Monterrey didn't seem to have a drinking age. Not a big drinker; I probably didn't order anything anyway. I remember standing around with a few other people who weren't much older than we were, enthralled by the music and the band.

After they played, we went to the stage area to meet them and try out our Spanish. I think they were flattered that we made the effort to speak their language. There were four of them, and they were old—must have been around 18 to my 14! They were cute and appeared to like having fans from New York. As for me, I was excited to be in their company!

We returned to the record shop the following week to buy one of their albums. The next time we went to the club, I took my album and asked them to autograph it, which they did. I was sure they would become as famous as the Beatles.

More than 50 years after that hot Mexican summer, I still speak Spanish whenever possible. My autographed Los Rockets album is carefully nestled on the shelf along with the Fab Four and other greats of the 'sixties.

From "Stall Warning" to "Froggles"

Had my father been on the Titanic, more than 1,000 people might have survived. He figured out that if water had been allowed to enter the ship's stern through the seacocks in the "watertight" compartments, it would have counter-balanced the water pouring into the damaged bow. This would have distributed the water evenly in the bottom of the ship. It would have reduced the ship's steep angle and rapid sinking, giving the two nearby vessels enough time to rescue the passengers.

Dad had an uncanny ability to find solutions in the exact opposite of what seemed obvious. No one on the Titanic thought to fill the stern with water.

My father was also an observer. That's partly how he came up with his Stall Warning Indicator, an instrument that keeps airplanes from stalling and possibly crashing. To quote from his book "Inventorship," "I find dozens in the aviation business in my backyard. They're birds…and they inspired my first invention, the Stall Warning Indicator. I learned that tiny hairs on their wings help sense the airflow over their wings when they fly, and the Stall Warning Indicator tells pilots the same thing about their wings."

My father could explain, fix, or create solutions for practically anything. Growing up, I took it for granted, although I knew my father was different from my friends' fathers. As a pilot and the inventor of aeronautical safety instruments, my father had an airplane. Once when we were flying back from a weekend trip, he said: "Watch this. See the runway ahead?"

It was daylight, and I was sitting in the co-pilot's seat; of course, I could see it. I wondered what was so unusual about that.

"Well," he continued, "I'm going to take my hands off the controls, and the plane is going to land itself with the automatic landing system I am inventing."

This was an actual test flight! I reminded myself that Dad was a member of the prestigious Society of Experimental Test Pilots (as was Randy), but I was still a little nervous. I watched him remove his hands from the wheel. I marveled as the King Air started to shift gently from side to side, lining up perfectly with the runway. It was amazing to see a hands-free landing, and I shared the pride and excitement of what Dad called his "inventorship." When we touched down, I happily mimicked his "Fooled 'em again!"

Reading the paper at the breakfast table, my father would comment on the news with his suggestions for improvements. One day, while Randy and I were having lunch at Dad's house, there was news of a fatal airplane crash: An Eastern Airlines flight had crashed while on approach to JFK. The accident was attributed to a sudden change in wind direction and speed, which caused the plane to lose control. Suddenly Dad got excited and announced that the crash could have been avoided. He and Randy talked about wind shear and other things I didn't understand, and by the end of breakfast, they had a plan. Off they went to Safe Flight to work on it. What they developed, the Wind Shear Detector, is now on planes worldwide and has saved countless lives. I am proud to have been there at its conception.

Dad and Randy after a successful test flight

That was many years after my dad invented the Stall Warning Indicator, which landed my father in the National Inventors Hall of Fame. The late senator and astronaut John Glenn presented my dad with the award, saying, "Leonard Greene is among American inventors who have changed our world in ways we can see every day of our lives."

My father, Inductee in the National Inventors Hall of Fame, with John Glenn

Dad ended up with more than 200 patents. All of them were driven by his will to create or improve something. Most of them I didn't know anything about.

It wasn't until after his death that I learned he had invented those chirping walk signs that allow the visually impaired to cross busy streets safely. My father took his friend Brian, who was blind, to Cape Canaveral to "watch" one of the earliest space launches. Brian loved being at the launch, and my always-curious father asked him what might make his daily life easier. After some thought, Brian answered that he and his guide dog had trouble crossing the busy streets in White Plains, where he lived. My father's response? He designed an audio signal to indicate when it was safe to walk.

I recently discovered an old article about my father in a local magazine. Brian's wife had written about his friendship with Brian. She noted that my father once let Brian "pilot his plane and land it." Brian said it was 'no big deal!'

Dad designed a three-dimensional chess game, but no one was smart enough to figure out how to play it. I used to fiddle with the pieces, but it remained an interesting (patented but not produced) knick-knack.

After I was married, Dad came up with an idea for underwater goggles that would allow swimmers to see much better than goggles on the market. He described the lens he'd invented, shaped like a frog's eye. I told him I had the perfect name: "Froggles." He patented them and paid me $100 for my contribution.

My father and I at Safe Flight, enjoying a work break.

Gaga

In high school, I was allowed to take the train and the subway to Gaga's apartment on the corner of East 79th and Park Avenue. A liveried doorman escorted me in the private elevator to the 18th floor.

To those outside our family, Gaga was Elsa Kahn Saks, whose husband, Joseph, was the son of the founder of Saks Fifth Avenue. Widowed when she was in her 40s, she was Phyllis' mother and became my grandmother when Phyllis and my father married. When Doug learned to talk, he called her Gaga, which she remained until she died in her early 90s.

On entering her duplex penthouse, my feet would sink into the plush beige carpeting in her living room. The room was filled with richly upholstered sofas, club chairs, and exquisite mahogany tables and led to a wraparound terrace and greenhouse. I loved to stand out there and look down on the city, so far below that the sirens and traffic were muted. At night, I took in the lit-up sky-scrapers with awe.

Bridie, Gaga's cook, served us dinner in the dining room, where we ate on fine china with gold flatware. I had never seen gold utensils, and I have never seen them since. I loved Bridie's cooking; she once made a chicken breast in a cream sauce that was so delicious that I asked for the recipe. She obliged, but I found the instructions way too complicated. By y the time I was married and hoping to make the dish, I gave up and threw the recipe out.

Over dinner, Gaga shared stories from her past. One was about the first time she rode in a car. Her family had a summer home at the shore in New Jersey, and they traveled there by train until they bought a car. It had no windows, and it took four hours to drive the 60 miles to Elberon. Gaga remembered wearing a net over her face to protect her from the dusty roads. Unusual at the time of this new invention, Gaga insisted on learning to drive it herself.

When Gaga was a teenager, she and her friends used to go to a friend's house after dances, where their friend's mother made the best sandwiches and snacks they had ever tasted. Little did they know then that, one day, millions of people would enjoy Hellman's mayonnaise—named after their friend's mother, Mrs. Hellman!

Sometimes Gaga would take me to the theater. Afterward, we would return to her apartment, and I would follow her up the winding staircase to the guest room. The sleep sofa had a thick mattress that seemed to embrace me as I fell asleep to the hum of the city below.

One night, Gaga and I went to see Agatha Christie's "The Mousetrap." Walking arm in arm as we exited the side door of the packed theater, I felt something jostling between our bodies. I looked down to see an arm and a gloved hand on the latch of Gaga's handbag. I grabbed the hand and turned to find a well-dressed elderly man. Before I could say anything, he ran off. Apparently, that was a pickpocket's ploy: to dress as a theatergoer leaving a show. I felt like a hero, but it happened so fast that Gaga didn't know I had saved the day.

When I was 16, Doug, Randy, Chucky, and I went to the Viola Wolff dances. That was where the rich, Jewish prep school kids mingled against a backdrop of Lester Lanin and a five-piece band. We all had dinner at Gaga's, and then we'd get dressed in our formal attire—tuxedos for the boys and me in one of the gowns Mommy had bought me—probably at Saks in White Plains. I guessed we were training for things to come: these dances were supposed to be a good place to meet an "acceptable" date. But I always felt awkward, like an observer. The four of us bumpkins from Chappaqua did not fit in. We stuck together, rarely danced, and couldn't wait to return to Gaga's.

We spent a week each summer at Ocean Beach Club in Elberon, New Jersey. Gaga referred to OBC as shorthand for "ostentatious but comfortable!"

Gaga with the family at Ocean Beach Club, Elberon, NJ

15 ½ by 33

When I was a sophomore in high school, Gaga arranged a summer job for me at Saks Fifth Avenue—in the landmark store on Fifth Avenue! I was assigned to work in the men's department on the first floor. I knew nothing about men's clothing, even though I lived with five brothers and a father. When it came to shirts, I quickly learned that if I asked, "Are you a 15 ½ by 33?" the answer was usually yes. I also discovered that I had a knack for selecting the perfect tie for every shirt. I felt confident helping the customers because most men didn't have strong preferences about a particular tie, and I liked putting together colors that blended well.

For all I knew, some of those men were colorblind, like Chucky. Before his freshman year at college, Chucky asked me to pin his socks together by color because he couldn't distinguish between brown, grey, or blue, and he didn't want to be embarrassed wearing mismatched socks.

It was a stress-free summer job. I loved the store's rich smell, the gorgeous clothes, and the luxurious wood paneling—even in the elevators. Sometimes Gaga would stop by to visit. I think she got a kick out of seeing me there—in the family business! I liked to imagine that my assignment in the men's department in Saks Fifth Avenue had been preordained.

Every morning I took the train from Chappaqua to the city wearing the same sleeveless "little black dress" that all the female employees were required to wear. By the end of the summer, I couldn't bear to look at it. The only other time I wore it was at Mommy's funeral three years later. Then I threw it out.

November 22, 1963

I don't know why we got out of school 20 minutes early each Friday, but I always looked forward to it. On that particular Friday night, there was a home basketball game that I was going to with friends. One of the older ones would pick me up since I didn't have a car, and my Junior license wouldn't allow me to drive at night anyway.

Our school was modern compared to most. Four wings connected by covered walkways surrounded a grassy quad. The entire place was on one level, with each classroom flanked on two sides by floor-to-ceiling windows, providing open views of hallways and the quad. We were instructed to sit under our desks with our hands over our heads whenever we had an air raid drill, but I knew that wouldn't protect me from being shredded to pieces by all the flying glass. The fear of an attack by Russia was not limited to our dinner conversations at home about fallout shelters.

We always returned to our homerooms during the last 10 minutes of school to wait for the dismissal bell. Suddenly, someone ran past our classroom yelling, "The President has been shot!"

The hum of conversation stilled. It had to be a mistake. Or maybe he was somehow grazed by a bullet. Kennedy was fine.

We kept hearing about former President Eisenhower: every meal and movement since he'd had his heart attack. I knew Kennedy had back pain from injuries he suffered in WWII, but the only visible sign of his discomfort was the rocking chair he favored.

I'm sure it's not bad," I murmured. "Probably shot in the toe." I wasn't worried about our young, healthy President John Fitzgerald Kennedy.

"Good, I hope he dies," came from the girl sitting at the desk behind mine. I turned in disbelief and asked her to repeat what she had just said. She nodded, her orange hair bobbing. "I hope he dies," she said. I vowed never to speak to her again.

When the bell rang, we pushed out of the room and hurried through the halls to the parking lot. I turned the corner of the main building and was amazed at what I saw. The lot was full — and motionless. Usually, juniors and seniors cleared out quickly, especially on Fridays. But today, they sat silently in their cars, many with the doors left open, students half in and half out. Nobody moved. Nobody talked. Mournful music from their radios filled the air. As I walked past one of the cars, the music stopped, and I heard, "The President is dead."

How could this be? Maybe it wasn't true. I needed to get home as soon as possible, where it was safe, where Presidents weren't killed.

As the cars began to file slowly out of the parking lot, I headed down the sidewalk toward my bus. A loudspeaker announced that all sports were canceled. Of course, they were. Who could even think about a basketball game? Who would want to go?

I ran from the bus stop into the house, where I rushed to find Mommy. There she was, sitting in front of the TV in the den. She was alone—no one else was home yet—and I saw her crying. She never cried. I only saw her cry when her father-in-law, her Poppy, died. I sat down next to her and put my arm around her shoulders. Her red-polished lips were turned down; I was not used to seeing her without a smile. I knew she didn't want me to see her cry, but she couldn't help it. It made me want to control my tears, which didn't come until later.

As my brothers and sisters got home from school, we all gathered on the couch and the floor, huddled around the TV, glued to the awful news. The family stayed together the entire weekend, watching until after the president's funeral. I had never seen a military funeral. I learned about the riderless horse with boots in the stirrups facing backward: this represents a fallen leader looking back on his troops for the last time.

Before the funeral, Jackie Kennedy and Robert Kennedy, the president's brother, flew home from Texas on Air Force One with the body of the President. When they arrived at Andrews Air Force Base, I watched the television as Jackie stepped out of the plane wearing the pink suit she had worn in the car when her husband was shot. I had a dress coat the same color pink that made me feel like Jackie when I wore it. Now Jackie's suit was splattered with blood. It surprised me to see her so unkempt because she always dressed impeccably. Then the reporter explained that she hadn't wanted to change out of her bloodstained clothes so the world could see what "they" had done to her husband.

Next came the coffin holding the body of our beloved president. I couldn't believe that such a vibrant man was now still. I admired the strength that Jackie and Robert, and Ted Kennedy showed during the funeral procession, walking behind the horse-drawn casket, their heads held high. So much black—the black limousines, the black clothes, the black veil covering Jackie's tears.

Two days later, Jack Ruby shot Lee Harvey Oswald in the stomach as he entered the hallway of the Dallas police station. As soon as I saw it happen, I ran out of the den and up the stairs to my parent's room. I barged into the bathroom, where my father was taking a bath. "They shot Oswald! I am happy that he killed the monster who killed Kennedy." I announced. I couldn't get over the fact that I had just seen a man killed on live TV.

My father disagreed. "That's terrible," he said. "Now, we will never know the truth about the assassination."

When the weekend was over, I saw pictures in newspapers and magazines from all over the world showing masses of people crying. The entire world was crying. No more President Kennedy. No more handsome couple in the White House. No more Camelot.

Postscript: Dad was right: We still don't know the truth about the assassination. And I never spoke to the girl with the orange hair again.

"Billie"

"Why?" my new stepbrothers asked. "Why do you call her Billie instead of Mom?"

After my father and Phyllis married, I experienced what it meant to have a "real" mother for the first time. From the start, even though she was my stepmother, I called Phyllis "Mommy" whenever I spoke to her or about her. I referred to my biological mother as "Billie."

Calling Billie my biological mother might have seemed cold, yet that was the only connection I felt to her. "You are so mean," Chucky, who was 13 then, concluded when I said I didn't want to go on a divorce-mandated weekend to see her in Massachusetts. Mommy heard Chucky's comment and suggested he go along with me. To my surprise, both he and Billie agreed.

The weekend was boring, except for one afternoon at a lake. Billie did not attempt to hide her disinterest in us the whole time. Chucky didn't say anything about it to me, but as soon as we got home, he went to Mommy, and I overheard him say, "I don't blame Bonnie for not wanting to see Billie!"

Not loving my mother always felt like a deficit on my part. I didn't understand her illness; I didn't even have a name for it. I remember her taking lots of medicine that made her breath bad and her mouth dry. But she no longer lived in a hospital. She didn't have operations or lose her hair. She looked healthy. What would make a mother not love her child? The unloved child must be unlovable. What was wrong with me that my mother, my so-called "real" mother, didn't care for me?

Randy and Laurie seemed to flounder between wanting her to be their mother and acknowledging that she never could be. Phyllis got pushed aside while they tried to handle their emotions. Loving Phyllis was not as easy for them as it was for me. I assumed it was because they didn't want to appear disloyal to Billie. I reasoned that it was not worth worrying about my loyalty towards Billie since she was unable or unwilling to worry about me.

For the rest of her life, Billie held a grudge against me for something I did as a senior in high school. I know this because, for years after the "incident," she repeatedly mentioned it to Laurie.

Billie lived in Ann Arbor with her second husband when I was college hunting. One of my options was the University of Michigan, so when a freshman friend there invited me to visit him for a weekend, I said yes. Sunday morning, as he and I were walking out of the Brown Jug, where apparently all of Ann Arbor went for brunch, I bumped into Billie, who was waiting to get in. I was startled; we hadn't spoken in years. I braced myself and, without thinking, introduced her to my friend as "Billie."

It had never occurred to me that I might see her. I had forgotten that she had moved there; if I had remembered, I doubt I would have tried to contact her. But Billie was insulted. Whenever she spoke to Laurie or Randy, they reported that the only comment she made about me was that I had offended her by introducing her as Billie and not my mother.

After Dad died, Randy went through his papers in his desk drawer at Safe Flight. Dad had a file of memorabilia that he had saved for us. In it was a note Billie had sent to Randy, thanking him for mailing her some photographs. It was handwritten, chatty, and thoughtful. She'd signed it "Billie."

CHAPTER FOUR

Deep Loss

Two years after Dad married Phyllis, she started to get sick. I was 13, and Terry was only one. My father told us that Mommy had to have a hysterectomy, but the word "cancer" was never mentioned.

When she returned from the hospital, Mommy continued to care for us as she always did. She even continued to work as a guidance counselor at the Rippowam Cisqua School for several years.

When I came home from school, I often found her sitting in the blue velvet club chair with her stockinged feet propped up on the ottoman. If she were reading a book or magazine, she'd put it down as soon as she saw me. She listened to me chatter away about whatever had happened in school. She always had time for me. She never complained about being sick, tired, or uncomfortable, so I thought everything was back to normal.

Occasionally our parents went away for a week; Dad told us they were on vacation. Once he said Mommy needed more surgery to remove the scar tissue from the first operation. Over time, I noticed that she seemed to go to doctor appointments more often. Years later, I found out a world-renowned radiologist saw her. Dad had begged him to treat Mommy's cancer with experimental gold beads in exchange for flying him to conferences (one as far as Brazil).

Still, I never suspected anything was wrong until I walked into Mommy's room when she was getting dressed and saw that her abdomen was bloated. She looked pregnant. I was confused, and I was upset.

"Why don't you go to a different doctor?" I asked. "Why don't you go to one who will make you better?"

She turned to me. "You should mind your own business," she told me. "Don't say that again."

Mommy had never spoken to me like that. She didn't have a bad temper, and I couldn't understand why she reacted that way when all I wanted was for her to improve.

For four more years, her stomach was bloated. I knew because she wore maternity dresses. Her dark brown hair turned gray at the temples, and she lost her eyelashes. Chucky and I shared our fears about Mommy; we whispered the word "cancer," but neither could believe it was possible. Meanwhile, our parents behaved as if everything were normal.

I started college at the University of Wisconsin in late August. When I asked my parents to come for Parents' Weekend in October, Mommy wrote back that they couldn't but would visit another time soon. A few days before Parents' Weekend, my father called to tell me that Mommy was in the hospital. He said she was very sick, but cancer was not mentioned. When I asked if I could come home, he said no.

I was terrified that Mommy might die. Barbara, a friend from Chappaqua, lived down the hall. I knew she was a devout Christian, so I asked her to help me pray for my mother. She sat with me on my bed, and as she prayed, I knelt and said, "Amen." Even though I am Jewish, I believed Christians had the edge in communicating with God, and I was desperate to try anything.

The following day, my father called. "Mommy asked for ice cream," he said. Relieved and furious at the same time, I said, "Don't ever scare me like that again!" We said goodbye, and I thought all was going to be okay.

But then, early the following day, Mrs. Wendt, our house-mother, climbed the three flights of stairs to my room to tell me I had a phone call. Our dorm switchboard didn't open until 7 AM, so the call had come in on her private line. "Who is it?" I asked as I hurried down the stairs behind her. "Is it a man?" Mrs. Wendt didn't answer.

Fear gripped my insides. She led me into her room and handed me the phone. It was Stevie, and as soon as I said hello, he said, "Dad wants to speak to you." Then I heard my father's voice: "Mommy died last night. You need to come home." I don't remember answering him.

I ran upstairs, borrowed an overnight case from Barbara, and packed the only black dress I owned, which I had worn each day when I worked at Saks. I asked Mrs. Wendt to call a taxi and rode to the airport in silence. Grabbing Barbara's white suitcase, I rushed to the gate and told the agent I had a family emergency and had to get on the next plane to New York. I didn't have a credit card and had no memory of paying for the flight. I flew North Central Airlines to Milwaukee, where I needed to take a Northwest flight to New York. I raced to the first gate in Milwaukee that said New York and repeated my distress to the agent, who put me on the plane. I am pretty sure I flew the whole way for no charge.

En route to New York, I sat in the front, with two seats facing me occupied by a middle-aged couple. I pressed my head against the window, looking out at the blue sky and white clouds, willing the plane to crash. The flight attendant asked me if I wanted anything, and I shook my head no. She kept asking, so I closed my eyes, hoping to be left alone. The couple across from me whispered, "These kids think they have problems." I wanted to scream at them. My whole world had just collapsed.

At JFK, I jumped into a taxi. I knew that if I told the driver I was going to Chappaqua, he would ask me to get out. Most people had never heard of Chappaqua, and I didn't know what I would do if I couldn't get a ride, so I said I lived in White Plains. I convinced him it wasn't too far from JFK. Then I directed him to Chappaqua and ran into the house, asking my uncle, the first person I saw, to pay the fare.

It took only four hours, door to door, to get home from Wisconsin – a record-breaking time. But as soon as I arrived, I stopped. I didn't know what to do next.

I was surprised to see that Gaga was already there, and I asked her when she had heard. I asked several other people the same question. They all told me they had known how sick Mommy was for a long time. I was shocked. How could they have known?

My father came downstairs from his bedroom, and as I watched him approach me, I was hit with a sudden sense of profound loss, mixed with an unexpected discomfort. At that moment, I didn't know how to relate to him. My love for my new mother overshadowed my relationship with the man who had once been my only parent. I wanted to be comforted, yet I realized he wouldn't be able to do that. He was too engrossed in his grief. I never asked him why he hadn't allowed me to come home to say goodbye to Mommy when he knew she was dying.

Dad arranged for a memorial service at the Ethical Culture Society on Mamaroneck Road in White Plains. There was no casket, no urn, just a tall glass vase with stringy yellow flowers placed on the floor. A stranger read a poem called "Dust to Dust," which she held on a piece of onionskin paper. I asked her for it and took it home to reread. It meant nothing to me and didn't comfort me at all. This was one thing Dad couldn't fix.

We all huddled emotionally and physically at the house, with nothing but sorrow. None of us could fathom why such a wonderful, kind, and loving person could be taken away from a family that was finally healing from the pain of our earlier lives. Terry was only six. I told my father I would transfer to a local college to help care for Terry, but he said no.

It was hard for me to believe that Phyllis, my beloved mother and my "Mommy," was dead. Well into my 30s, I would think I spotted her in crowds, and I often dreamt that she came back, but she didn't. Phyllis Freeman Greene died on October 21, 1965.

Mommy and me

CHAPTER FIVE

Madison, Wisconsin

Mad about Madison

I went to the University of Wisconsin because I didn't get into Michigan. That ended up being a good thing. Except for the cold and windy winters, Madison was a wonderful place to go to school. The campus bordered Lake Mendota, which is large and beautiful, where students could take sailing lessons, go ice fishing, or sit on the terrace at the Rathskeller (student union) and enjoy the view.

Although there was usually something more interesting to do, I went to classes and studied. My major was Latin American studies with a minor in art history. My goal was to join the Peace Corps and live somewhere in South America, doing precisely what I didn't know. The art history minor was for pure joy.

By the time I was a junior, I had decided that school wasn't keeping me busy enough, so I took a part-time job at the radio station on campus. WHA was a National Public Radio station, the oldest station in the country. I was assigned to the recording lab with no background or interest in radio other than listening to rock 'n roll. Sitting at my desk each week, I watched news reporters put together and read the news. With his smooth baritone voice, I heard Ken Graham present "Chapter A Day," the original book, on tape. WHA also made public service announcements, and I was sometimes allowed to be part of those productions. Once, helping with the sound effects, I shook a rice can to simulate hail. After a while, I asked if I could write ads for the Madison Public Library, and I was told to give it a try. I wrote some humorous scripts, and they were accepted. It was hard for me to believe they were good enough until I heard them on the radio.

What I liked the most about working at WHA was meeting the politicians who frequently came to Madison to stir up voters. As part of the recording department, I helped bring equipment wherever a media event occurred.

Over the years, the list of visitors included Jacob Javits, Eugene McCarthy, Ted Kennedy, and Hubert Humphrey. I met William Proxmire at the Wisconsin State Fair, telling him I would drop out of college to work for his Presidential campaign. He gave me an appropriate fatherly hug and told me to stay in school. Another time I told a young John Kerry that he should run for President. He responded with a friendly letter saying it wasn't his time.

WRIGHT PATMAN, TEX., CHAIRMAN
RICHARD BOLLING, MO.
HALE BOGGS, LA.
HENRY S. REUSS, WIS.
MARTHA W. GRIFFITHS, MICH.
WILLIAM S. MOORHEAD, PA.
WILLIAM B. WIDNALL, N.J.
W. E. BROCK 3D, TENN.
BARBER B. CONABLE, JR., N.Y.
CLARENCE J. BROWN, OHIO

JOHN R. STARK,
EXECUTIVE DIRECTOR

WILLIAM PROXMIRE, WIS., VICE CHAIRMAN
JOHN SPARKMAN, ALA.
J. W. FULBRIGHT, ARK.
HERMAN E. TALMADGE, GA.
STUART SYMINGTON, MO.
ABRAHAM RIBICOFF, CONN.
JACOB K. JAVITS, N.Y.
JACK MILLER, IOWA
LEN B. JORDAN, IDAHO
CHARLES H. PERCY, ILL.

JAMES W. KNOWLES,
DIRECTOR OF RESEARCH

Congress of the United States

JOINT ECONOMIC COMMITTEE

(CREATED PURSUANT TO SEC. 5(a) OF PUBLIC LAW 304, 79TH CONGRESS)

WASHINGTON, D.C. 20510

December 9, 1970

Bonnie LeVar
511 West Mifflin St.
Madison, Wisconsin 53703

Dear Bonnie:

Thanks so much for your letter.

I share your concern over the events reported on the CBS program concerning Safari Island.

Although legislation has passed the Senate during this session to protect endangered species of wildlife, only certain species were included. It may well be necessary for the Senate to take a good hard look at this problem with a view toward more stringent legislation.

In the meantime, I have forwarded your letter to the Interior Department and have asked them to advise me what may be done about this matter. As soon as I have received a reply from them I will be in touch with you again.

Sincerely,

William Proxmire, U.S.S.

WP:ssa

Corresponding with Senator William Proxmire

WILLIAM PROXMIRE
WISCONSIN

United States Senate

WASHINGTON, D.C. 20510

May 6, 1971

Mrs. John LeVar
661 Mendota Ct.
Madison, Wis.

Dear Mrs. LeVar:

You are most gracious to express your support for me
as a potential candidate for the Presidency.

There's an outside chance that I might run, and you're
wonderful to offer your encouragement.

Sincerely,

William Proxmire, U.S.S.

WP:prc

511 West Mifflin
April 1968

During this time, I lived with two girls, Lyn and Joyce. We shared the first floor of an old rundown house, pale green with a large front porch. It was on Mifflin Street, catty-corner to the center of hippie-dom, anti-war protests, the People's Park, and the food co-op.

My bedroom was a small room next to the kitchen, and Lyn and Joyce shared a bedroom in the back. Two other girls lived in the apartment upstairs. Lyn and Joyce's room had a door that led to a patchy backyard and gravel driveway. Since we didn't have cars and never used that door, Joyce's bed blocked it.

One April afternoon, when I was studying alone in the apartment, I heard a knock on the back door. I ignored it. Whoever was knocking knocked again. I looked out the window for a car or a bike in the driveway, but I didn't see anything.

The next thing I heard was the back door opening and the sound of the bed rolling over the linoleum floor. Barefoot and terrified, I hopped off the couch and flew out the front door. The street was empty, and I didn't know what to do.

Then I spotted someone walking in my direction. He stopped and watched as I paced frantically in front of my apartment. He carried a Doors album under his arm and looked like a fellow student. "Do you need help?" he asked.

I nodded yes, but immediately worried that he might be a lookout for whoever was inside the house. This is crazy, I thought. Still, I didn't know what to do. "Will you go in and look?" I asked, aware that he was a stranger, but I was desperate. He agreed and opened the door. I waited on the sidewalk, ready to run for it.

I heard a girl's voice on the other side of the door. Deeming it safe, I went back in to see what was happening. My "hero" was standing in the doorway facing the girl. I was right behind him and couldn't understand why it was one of the girls who lived upstairs. She told me that she had been studying in the backyard and lost a contact; she wondered if we had a flashlight.

It didn't occur to me until later that it was sunny outside, and a flashlight was unnecessary. Another thing that seemed off was that no one ever used the backyard—there were no chairs or tables—so why had she been studying out there? Before I could even open a drawer to search for a flashlight, she announced, "Never mind, I found my contact."

I was stunned when I realized that our upstairs neighbor – a housemate and, I thought, a friend—had been planning to rob our apartment. I can only surmise that she was looking for cash or drugs—neither of which was present. She never apologized or explained, and I had nothing to do with her for the rest of the semester.

Meanwhile, I didn't know what to do with the stranger who had offered to "rescue" me. I did notice his good looks—chiseled chin, brown hair, hazel eyes, muscular build—but I was clueless about what to do or say next.

That was when he saw the book I had dropped when I heard the back door open. It was in Portuguese: Part of my plan to join the Peace Corps in South America was to learn Portuguese. We introduced ourselves, and I discovered that John was born in Brazil and could help teach me the language.

Later, when I called my father to tell him what had happened, he said, "He should have never gone into the house. He should have taken you to dinner and told you to call your insurance agent!"

April and May

That was the beginning of a series of unsettling events in Madison.

One of my first dates with John was to hear Otis Redding at a club called The Factory. That afternoon, the radio kept reporting a small plane crash in nearby Lake Monona. The story was odd because they kept repeating that a lot of money was floating in the water. Eventually, it was revealed that the passenger was Otis Redding. I was too upset to get a refund, but I wish I had kept the ticket as a memento. I still cannot hear "Sitting on the Dock of the Bay" without thinking about that day. "Two thousand miles I roam, just to make this dock my home...." John and I went to a movie for our first date, but not that night. It was too sad to think of Otis Redding's death in our lake.

The 1960s in Madison were years of anti-war protests. It was not unusual to see police and students facing off. Sometimes at night, the police hovered over our street in helicopters with strobe lights lighting up the block as if it were noon on a sunny day. I'd looked out my window to watch students scatter so the police on the ground couldn't arrest them. Although I staunchly opposed the war in Viet Nam, I remained an observer, not a protester. Still, it was hard to avoid the fumes when the protests became unwieldy, and the crowds were tear-gassed. The bitter sting of the gas in my eyes and mouth was painful, and the only antidote was time.

I loved art history and took every class I could fit into my schedule. One day I was walking to my favorite class in the basement of Bascom Hall. Bascom Hall was in the center of campus, where the President's office was located. It was also at the top of a hill, and you could tell how many classes someone had in Bascom by the size of their calf muscles. I had many classes up the hill, and I still have the legs to prove it.

That day, as I approached Bascom, I saw the building surrounded by National Guardsmen. I had to pass through them to enter. I gingerly walked between two men who had their rifles out—with bayonets attached. The men looked straight ahead. I felt nauseous. I walked into my classroom, but the beauty of the paintings on the screen was not enough to erase the thought of the guns outside. Had I been a protester, what would they have done to me?

The National Guard and armed police were not the only signs of violence simmering in Madison. A few weeks after our upstairs neighbor's break-in, I was in the living room when Lyn came running out of her room, screaming that someone had tried to get into our apartment again. The blood had drained from her already pale face. She had been asleep when she heard the door opening, she told us, and then she saw a man in a yellow shirt standing in the doorway. In her naturally husky voice, Lyn asked, "Who's there? and the man took off. She was so scared that if she hadn't set her long blonde hair in rollers, I am sure it would have been standing straight up. As for me, I jumped into the hall closet and tried to hide behind a guitar. When we calmed down, we called the police, and from then on, they routinely circled our block.

Shortly after our second aborted break-in, there was a murder in Madison. Christine Rothschild of the famous Rothschild family was found stabbed to death on campus. She was on her way to church. Students began walking to classes in groups. I didn't feel safe until my father flew to Madison to take me home when the semester was over.

I lived in a large dormitory closer to my classes during my senior year.

The year after that, I married my rescuer, John LeVar, with whom I share a son, a daughter, four grandchildren, and more than fifty years of marriage.

Christine Rothschild's killer was never found but was suspected of being involved in several murders in Madison over the next decade. I sometimes wonder if he was the man in the yellow shirt.

CHAPTER SIX

Even a Genius
Can Make a Mistake

A little more than a year after Mommy died, I came home from college for a long weekend. Walking in the front door, I was surprised to find the blonde woman who was dating my father standing in the foyer. She was talking with another woman who held a clipboard under her arm as she examined a Chinese porcelain bowl set on a small mahogany table. The bowl had belonged to Mommy.

I was not introduced to the woman, who, I realized, was discussing the bowl's value. I glanced at her clipboard and saw a list of items I could tell had been appraised.

I had met the blonde woman standing in the foyer years earlier when she and her husband joined my father and Mommy on our sailboat for a day on the Long Island Sound. Donny and I were there, along with the woman's young daughter, who did nothing but whine and cry. Every time she started in, her mother would coddle her and feed her pretzels, which didn't accomplish anything.

Later, in the privacy of our car, Mommy turned to my father and said, "I have never seen such a terrible mother." I couldn't believe it: She had never talked about people like that. She had, unwittingly validated my opinion of the woman.

After Mommy died, Laurie, still living at home, told me there was a plentiful supply of (not too subtle) women circling my wealthy father. There was my Dad, in despair over the death of Phyllis and confused as to how to go on now—now with eight children. I believe he ended up marrying the blonde because she had the advantage of having known him socially before Mommy died. She quickly divorced her husband (from whom she was separated) and let my father know that she was up for anything —tennis, skiing, boating. After five years of living with a woman battling ovarian cancer, Dad probably wanted to make what must have seemed a healthy choice for someone to take care of six-year-old Terry. I wish I had reminded him of Mommy's assessment of the blonde's parenting.

Actually, I tried. Dad asked each of us, one at a time, if he should marry her. When it was my turn, I said no as firmly as possible. I later consulted with my siblings and learned that my view was shared unanimously.

A few months later, he married her.

John and I lived in Pleasantville, the town next to Chappaqua, and I would fetch Terry, who spent as much time as possible at our house.

It was only when he was dying that my father admitted that marrying her was a mistake. He had hoped that the nicer he was to her, the more she would change. He was wrong. She never did.

Fear of Flying

My fear of flying was the one exception to my belief in my father's magical protective powers. As a small child, I didn't have a choice, but after my own children were born, I refused to fly anywhere for nine years.

Never one to give up, my father thought of a way to get me back in an airplane. He told Donny to take me across the street to the Safe Flight hangar and bring out the Beechcraft, a four-seater. Donny did, and once there, he said that Dad would give me $20 if I could stay in the plane, with the propellers spinning, for 15 minutes. My father went as far as to have someone from Safe Flight stand on the tarmac and time us. Inside the plane, chuckling at the absurdity of our situation, Donny and I decided to see how much more Dad would pay to "cure" me.

When we returned to the office, we told him it was tough and that I needed more training (and more money for more time). Dad wasn't that gullible, but Donny and I thought it was hilarious.

Real as it was, my fear of flying made no sense to my father or me. His fix didn't work, but cognitive behavioral therapy helped to get me back in the air again. The real magic was my love for Jonathan and Joanie. I didn't want to disappoint them any longer by forcing them to miss "Poppy's" family trip to Club Med every year for Turkey Week.

SMITH INSTRUMENT CORP
BERMUDA
NEW YORK

CHAPTER SEVEN

Moving On

Turkey Week

Dad's new wife hated Thanksgiving. She did not attempt to hide the fact that it was nothing but an inconvenience to have to put up with all of Dad's children at the same time and to sit together—all twelve of us, plus spouses and grandchildren—for a meal. There were employees to help clean and cook the traditional turkey. Yet, that was her none-too-subtle attempt to prove that she (and not the cook) had slaved over a frozen turkey for an hour or two. On our way to the house for Thanksgiving each year, we stopped at Burger King so Jonathan and Joanie wouldn't go hungry!

After a few years of this unpleasant "holiday," my father accepted her proposal to have Thanksgiving dinner elsewhere. The deal? My father would treat all of us (usually about 50) to a week at a Club Med for Thanksgiving. And so, from the early 1980s until just before his death, he took us to different resorts each Thanksgiving. We called it Turkey Week.

My siblings lived as far away as Chucky in California, Laurie in Montana, Randy in Colorado, and as close as Donny in Greenwich, Connecticut. It was one of the rare times we were all together in one place. We stayed at every Club Med that had a children's club, and I was grateful that I had been able to overcome my fear of flying so that Jonathan and Joanie wouldn't miss all the fun. John and I looked forward to this annual gathering, and our children couldn't wait to be with their many cousins. Club Med usually has an open seating arrangement for their guests, but they reserved five tables of ten for us because we wanted to sit together as a family.

Turkey Week at Club Med Bonnie, Jonathan, Joan, and John

Part of our ritual became the family T-shirts we designed for each location. When our trip to Guadeloupe was almost canceled one year because of Hurricane Lenny, our father – the original Leonard – created a Hurricane Lenny @ Guadeloupe motif, which we all wore proudly.

My father planned our final Turkey Week, knowing it would be his last, but we never went because he ended up in the hospital. He died a few days after Thanksgiving.

Donny and I in Bermuda for Turkey Week

John and I at a fundraiser in the '70s

In the Meantime

John and I were married a year after I graduated from the University of Wisconsin. We rented an apartment on Garth Road in Scarsdale, and when we were ready to start our family, we bought a small house on Mountain Road in Pleasantville. That's the house Terry used as a refuge from Dad's third wife, and I loved having her around.

Jonathan and Joanie were born soon after our move to Pleasantville, and a few years later, we bought a larger house in Briarcliff. It was down the street from Doug and his family, so Jonathan and Joanie spent much time with them. It was also only 10 minutes from the Chappaqua house, so we often got together with my dad, whom the kids called "Poppy." Being so close meant we spent many summers swimming and barbequing in Poppy's backyard. And we always looked forward to our annual Turkey Week reunions.

Poppy introduced Jonathan and Joanie to many of the activities I enjoyed as a kid, taking them to plays and going sailing or skiing. A few times he flew us all to his house in Fort Lauderdale. (His wife would spend the week in Vermont or somewhere else when we went to Florida).

John and I resurrected one of my favorite childhood activities with our kids: While we ate dinner, we took turns reading riddles from the "Seven Minute Mystery" series. We had almost as much difficulty solving them as I had had with the missionaries and cannibals. And we had just as much fun.

Jonathan and John shared a love of running. While John focused on long-distance runs—he ran the New York and Marine Corps marathons—Jonathan ran track, breaking the school record in the 800-yard events. Joanie participated in tennis, soccer, and most school activities. She was an avid reader, often reading herself to sleep at bedtime; her friends nicknamed her "Miss Page Turner." Joanie's other obsession was Garfield. Her bedroom at home remains a shrine to him, with her bed lined with all sizes of the funny cat.

Joan, John, Bonnie & Jonathan

And then there are our dogs. For the past 40 years, we have shared our home with a series of beautiful English Cocker Spaniels. I can't imagine my life without them—which might have been a possibility had Dad not taken care of my fear of dogs early on.

"Oscar," our newest English Cocker Spaniel

AGPO

Turkey Week was great, but we were a huge bunch, with siblings and step-siblings, brothers- and sisters-in-law, nieces, nephews, and grandchildren. AGPO gave a smaller group of us the chance to spend quality time with Dad.

One year, Dad invited only his daughters and granddaughters to go on a trip with him. We were going to be "All Girls Plus

One"—lovingly dubbed AGPO. We ordered T-shirts: a sky blue background with a rainbow of colors and AGPO splashed across the front in large letters. Laurie had matching AGPO pins made up for the occasion.

Our first trip was a four-day sail down the Intercoastal Waterway from Norfolk, Virginia, to Beaufort, North Carolina, on "Windshear," Dad's 72-foot sailboat. It would include Laurie, Terry, Beth, Stevia, Joanie, and me. The boat had enough bunks to accommodate us except for Terry, who managed to sleep on the floor between us.

Before the trip, we were told to list all our favorite foods for our sail. We wrote our separate wish lists, which we gave to Dad, who had the boat stocked with our requests. Once under sail, we decided to check the provisions for lunch. Ice cream was the runaway favorite. We had more ice cream than a Ben & Jerry's franchise. I will never forget Laurie with her head and torso down the hatch, searching for her favorite flavor. All that was visible were her long legs sticking straight up in the air!

"Windshear" had a 60-foot mast. This was not of any particular interest to me until we approached the first of the many bridges we had to sail under. We checked the navigation map, which was used to alert sailors to river depths and bridge heights, we found that our first bridge was 60 feet 3 inches. We had to glide in the exact center of the bridge and pray that the tide would not interfere with our plans to keep the mast. In hindsight, I am sure Dad knew exactly what he was doing. However, we all held our breath, which became the routine for the rest of the bridges along the Intercoastal Waterway.

Sailors are friendly people. I loved traveling along the Waterway with the same group of boats around us. It was incredibly relaxing, floating quietly by marshes, little towns, native trees, and water birds. We'd exchange a wave with the people on a boat we'd passed the day before and say hello with another traveler on the way up the river. A boat would sometimes glide by with a dog standing at the bow. I was envious until I imagined that my English Cocker would probably have fallen or jumped in!

Being with Dad—without cell phones and interruptions—was the most special part. We got up in the morning, sat on the deck in our pajamas, and ate breakfast. I don't remember anything except the abundance of ice cream, but we must have had some appropriate breakfast food. In his pale blue pajamas with navy piping, Dad strummed his ukulele and tried to accompany us while we tried to sing.

We ate our dinners at local restaurants on piers along the way. On Sunday, we went for brunch at a "fancy" restaurant in Beaufort. A basket of corn fritters, which I had never tasted, was placed on the table. They were warm, buttery, and irresistible. Laurie caught me surreptitiously wrapping up all the uneaten fritters in a cloth napkin and stuffing them into my pocketbook.

One might think we were a family of sailors, but that was not the case for our AGPO group. Terry and I are prone to seasickness. Laurie lives on a farm in Montana and rarely sails. The appeal of this particular AGPO was being with Dad.

Not to mention the fact that he promised us the Intercoastal Waterway would be smooth as glass. It was. He neglected to tell us that the middle of our trip would include crossing Albemarle

Sound. I couldn't believe it. Suddenly it looked like we were in the middle of the ocean! You could barely see the shore.

Although we were on a sailboat, the entire trip until this point had been under power. No sails. Following Dad's instructions, we unfurled the sails and navigated across the sound. I felt the wind slapping my face and tugging at my hair. It was like we were flying. It was fabulous!

Trimming the sails with Joanie

We decided to put down anchor for the night at the other end of the sound. The moon and stars were reflected on the water, and we had to peer into the darkness for a buoy where we could tie up. Laurie came to the rescue. She took a lantern and held it out as far as she could without falling into the water, searching for and finding the buoy.

We continued our leisurely trip down the waterway the next day until we reached the last bridge. There was Donny, signaling us from the bridge. He had flown down to meet us and take us to the airport for our trip home.

We were all up on the deck waving to Donny when we hit a sandbank. Must have happened often, because towboats were lined up, waiting for us and the others who planned to dock there, ready to bring us all in for a hefty fee.

Dad and his "crew" on "Windshear"

Introductions Not Necessary

The last person I wanted to see when I agreed to attend my Uncle Larry's funeral was my biological mother, Billie. Still, she stood in front of a mirror in the foyer, adjusting her coarse salt-and-pepper hair. My uncle was Billie's brother. I was already married and in my 40s when he died after a long illness, and in keeping with Jewish tradition, his burial was scheduled for the next day. When Larry's wife, my Aunt Joan, called to give me details about the funeral, I asked her if Billie would be there because I thought it would be highly uncomfortable for both of us if I were there, too.

My aunt assured me that my mother would not make it; she was in Vermont, spending the summer taking a writing course. So, I decided to go, and I arranged with my aunt to come to her house to drive to the service together.

That's where I ran into my mother, the first person I saw when I entered the house. I wondered how she had gotten there so quickly; I wished she'd remained in Vermont. However, this was her brother's funeral, and her attendance took priority over mine. I considered leaving but decided I would stay.

She turned away from the mirror to greet me. "I'm Larry's sister," she announced and held out her hand.

I froze, absorbing her words. Then I looked directly into her eyes, lifted my hand to shake hers, and responded, "And I am your daughter."

I hoped she might say something to remove the hurt of her introduction, but she dropped my hand and walked away.

Behind me, my cousin Leslie burst into tears.

I hated that the exchange had upset Leslie, who was already grieving the loss of her father. I was there for my aunt and my cousins. "I'm so sorry you had to see that," I told her.

Nonetheless, another part of me felt consoled that Leslie had witnessed my mother's behavior and seemed to be as shaken as I was. I couldn't stop replaying the moment. What had my mother been thinking? How was it possible that she hadn't recognized me? I looked the same as I always did—like her mother, my Grandma Betty. I don't remember much of the funeral. I spent the day trying to avoid Billie, and she did not attempt to speak to me.

The minute I got home, I called Randy. Of course, Billie had recognized me, he said. "She was only posturing."

Posturing, yes. His explanation relieved me: at least she knew who I was. But the incident has never left me: the oddness of it, the callousness and cruelty, Billie's utter absence.

Corporate Angel Network

It was December 1981, and the press was waiting for the plane to land at the Detroit airport. When it did, my father helped Michael, a 24-year-old with bone cancer, climb down the four steps and onto the tarmac. A loudspeaker started to play "I'll Be Home for Christmas." "There wasn't a dry eye in the house," Dad said.

That was the inaugural Corporate Angel Network flight, and Safe Flight was the first company to join CAN, as it is known. My dad co-founded CAN, whose mission was, and remains, to reduce the physical, emotional, and financial stress related to cancer patients' long-distance travel to and from treatment. After 40 years, CAN has partnered with over 500 U.S. corporations that have donated the use of their private planes for more than 64,000 cancer patient flights.

Because of the risk of infection associated with crowded commercial travel, Michael's only option to get from New York's Memorial Sloan Kettering to his home in Michigan would have been to drive. Michael and his family were grateful for the flight, which allowed him to be with them for Christmas during a hiatus in his treatment.

During the 20 years I spent at CAN, as President, Executive Director, and volunteer, I witnessed the courage displayed by patients of all ages and their families, with their optimism and willingness to travel repeatedly across the country for clinical trials. The host companies impressed me with their generosity in allowing strangers to share the limited seating on corporate jets and in making detours to pick up or drop off patients. Sometimes, if a flight fell on a child's birthday, the host corporation would provide pizza and a birthday cake, maybe stuffed animals or toys for the child, and there would be an instant party! The corporations did not ask for or want publicity about their philanthropic activities.

I never forgot that CAN's work was our way to honor Mommy and far too many others. My connection with the patients was extraordinary in other ways. Although they never knew it, I, too, was a cancer patient. A few years after I started working at CAN, I was diagnosed with CLL (Chronic Lymphocytic Leukemia). I was frightened by the diagnosis and worried about tolerating treatments. Witnessing the positive attitudes of the many patients we helped to get to treatment was a reminder that cancer is not necessarily a death sentence. Their bravery and hope served as a model for me. CAN was an unwitting support group, and I have tried to pay it forward when speaking with others.

CHAPTER EIGHT

September 11, 2001

Donald Freeman Greene

"…plane hit the World Trade Center." Turning toward the TV, which was on while I dressed, I stopped to listen more carefully. I looked at the screen and saw a small hole in the side of the building. *It must be a private plane*, I thought. The announcer continued to say that it was a commercial airliner. That wasn't possible, I reasoned because the hole was too small.

I stopped and called Donny. Not only was he a pilot, but he was someone whose opinion I valued. I knew he would assure me not to panic. As I waited for him to pick up, I remembered he was flying to a conference in New Orleans. Claudette answered instead, and I asked, "Has he gone already?"

"Yes," she replied, and I said goodbye.

Next, I called my father—also a pilot and just as capable as Donny of clearing this up. How could an airliner put a hole in the World Trade Center? His wife answered, and I asked to speak to Dad. "He can't come to the phone now. What do you want?"

"A plane flew into the World Trade Center!" I told her.

"Well, what do you want him to do about it?"

I hung up.

I finished dressing and watched angrily as a second plane flew around the building. *How did a plane get there quickly enough to take pictures?* I muttered out loud. *Sometimes the press is too much.*

Then I saw it slam into the building. It wasn't a news plane, and this was no accident. This was a terrorist attack!

Whenever there was a catastrophic aviation event, I did a mental checklist of my family to make sure they were all safe. Randy, Donny, and Dad were pilots and often flew because of their jobs. I remembered that Randy wasn't flying that day, and Dad was at home. The news reported that the airliner was en route to California, and Donny was going to New Orleans. I was relieved.

John was at an early dentist appointment, and I didn't want to stay home alone. There was no television at work, so I drove to my friend's house a few blocks from mine and rushed into her den, where I found I was not the only one who needed company that morning. Two other friends were already sitting in front of the TV. All I could think was that we must have lost members of our community who worked at the World Trade Center. I dreaded hearing the names of the casualties.

Then they showed a picture of a steel bridge in Pittsburgh. It was announced that a third plane had been hijacked. It had turned around as it passed over Pittsburgh and was headed toward Washington, DC. Horrified, I thought we would have to shoot it down before it reached its target—either the White House or the Capitol.

The morning went by in a blur. Images of the planes replayed on the television, and we sat in shock and rage that such a thing could have happened.

Then my cell phone rang. It was around 11 o'clock. Peter, a close friend from work, asked, "Where are you?"

I told him, and he said that he had to talk to me and would come over. "No," I said, "just tell me what you have to say." An elderly employee had had a health scare, and I guessed he had died. That was what I thought as I told Peter to tell me.

"Donny was on one of the planes."

"No!" I screamed. "No!" I hurled the phone across the room. I buried my head in the couch cushions, wanting to die.

Peter came to get me and drove me to Donny's house, where some of the family had already gathered. Randy, Doug, Chuck, and Steve were stuck in California because all commercial and private planes were grounded. Laurie was home in Montana. Terry was driving down from Boston. Dad was there, sitting alone at the kitchen table, all the color drained from his face. His wife was not there.

Then I saw Charlie, only ten years old, and he smiled and asked me why I was there. Jody, six, was running around and, like Charlie, seemed unaware of what was happening. I wondered what Claudette had told them about their father. She signaled to me that she had told them, so I decided that, understandably, they were in shock. The family continued to arrive until the kitchen was crowded. Cousins who hadn't seen each other in ages hugged and spoke softly. We were trying to comprehend the incomprehensible.

I was mistaken. Donny was flying to join his brothers on a hiking trip scheduled for the week before the conference in New Orleans. Why had he agreed to go? I wished he had missed the plane.

Some memories of that day are ingrained in my mind. My cousin's prediction: "This is a day that will change the world forever." The declaration from my father's attorney and close friend of Donny: "I truly loved your brother." He hugged me and sobbed on my shoulder.

A phone call later confirmed that Donald Freeman Greene was aboard United Flight 93, which had nosedived into a wildflower field in Shanksville, Pennsylvania. After listening to the voice recorder on the hijacked plane, it was reported that the passengers and crew had wrested the controls at the last minute and diverted the aircraft from hitting the elementary school that was in its flight path. The hijackers' original target was the U. S. Capitol, which was in full session at the time, as was the school.

The Next Week

Later, my father, broken-hearted, went home with his wife, who had finally arrived in the late afternoon. She had no words of comfort for Claudette or any of us. All I remember her saying was, "Have you heard from United yet?" I had always felt she was cold, but I was amazed by her ability to remove herself from our pain—and even from my father's.

Terry and I were the only siblings able to stay with Claudette, Charlie, and Jody; we slept in their guestroom for a week. Being with them during those days was the only place I wanted to be. In Donny's house. With his beautiful children.

During the day, friends and local relatives came to grieve with us. An aura of shock hung in the air. We tried to hold Charlie and Jody close at night, telling stories about their wonderful father. We did our best to control our tears, which were never far from falling. We started every meal by holding hands and saying a prayer that ended, "…and God bless Daddy." Claudette continued the tradition until Charlie and Jody were in high school.

After the children went to bed, Terry, Claudette, and I stayed awake, and together we grieved openly. We also drank a lot of wine, which didn't do much except make it easier to fall asleep.

A memorial was held at Temple Sholom in Greenwich as soon as the rest of the family could fly east. Putnam Avenue was closed, and a police motorcade helped mourners arrive and park. There were over 1,200 attendees. There was no casket.

Months later, Claudette was sent Donny's leather wallet, which had been recovered intact near the crash site. It contained pictures of Charlie and Jody.

White House Visit

After planes were allowed to fly again, President Bush invited the families of the passengers and crew of Flight 93 to the White House on September 21st. I was uncomfortable because I feared he would explain to us (before announcing to the public) that he had no choice but to shoot down the plane. I remembered that I had the same thought when watching the news at my friend's house. Would I have wanted to shoot it down if I had known my brother was on board?

I braced myself, but that is not what happened when we got to the White House. About 100 family members gathered in a formal room on the second floor and waited for the President to address the group. President and Mrs. Bush entered the room, and as they walked past me, Mrs. Bush stopped and squeezed my shoulder. "I'll see you later in the Blue Room," she said. I didn't know what she was talking about, so I simply nodded.

The President made some remarks but had trouble finishing them without crying. I don't remember much of what he said other than his recognition of the passengers' courage and patriotism. He then met individually with each family in the Blue Room next door, inviting us to spend as much time as we needed to speak with him. Most of my family was silent, probably overwhelmed at the thought of a private session with the President of the United States. Not me. I asked him what he would do to ensure this would never happen again. I said I wanted revenge. He said revenge was not the answer, but I wasn't satisfied with that. I wanted those responsible for the terrorist attack on our country found and tortured. At that point, Joan, my then-22-year-old daughter, said, "Mom, you're taking too much time with the President." President Bush put his arm around Joan's shoulders conspiratorially and smiled. "Don't worry," he said. "I'm 55, and my mother still embarrasses me all the time!" For the first time that day, we laughed.

The family of Donald F. Greene was invited to the White House to visit with President and Mrs. George W. Bush after the September 11th attacks.

After meeting with the president, each family was ushered through a side door that led to a small dining room. Several large round tables were set with pitchers of iced tea and platters of cookies. French doors opened onto a magnificent view of the White House lawn and the Washington Memorial. I welcomed the opportunity to stand alone in the September sunlight and have a moment to myself.

Exiting the White House, I was stunned at the sight of a long corridor lined on both sides with staffers holding American flags. As we walked through their path, they reached out and touched us gently, saying, "Thank you," and "God bless you." I looked down and tried not to cry. I appreciated their kindness, but I couldn't help thinking, "Don't thank me for the heroism of my brother as if it were my choice."

CHAPTER NINE

My Father's Final Flight

My Last Birthday with Dad

One of my lunch visits with Dad fell on my birthday; however, I didn't expect him to remember. Even before his lung cancer diagnosis, his secretary, Mary, would have to remind him of each of our birthdays. She wrote them on his large desk calendar, and if he were in the office that day, he would call to sing "Happy Birthday." I wished he'd remember mine, but I was used to it, and I knew it wasn't because he didn't care.

On this birthday, as I often did during the last months of my father's life, I left work at noon and headed to his home to have lunch with him. After he and his wife finally separated, he moved into a ranch house in Mamaroneck so he wouldn't have to negotiate steps. A few weeks earlier, I had been shocked to see his caretaker, Galena, pushing him out of his bedroom in a wheel-chair. I had never seen him use even a cane, and I didn't know he owned a wheelchair. Dressed in a navy-blue velour warm-up suit with a white polo shirt, my father, once six feet tall, was thin and stooped over in the chair. The twinkle was missing from his powder-blue eyes. I smiled and bent down to kiss his cheek, willing myself not to cry at his undeniable frailty. I pretended not to notice anything different in his appearance and didn't mention the wheelchair; I tried to convince myself that it was a good idea, preventing him from falling and keeping him from getting tired while walking around the small house. Galena told me he didn't always use it. But from then on, I couldn't deny how very fragile he was.

On my birthday visit, celebrating wasn't on my mind because I was so devastated by my father's declining health. Dad was waiting for me on the couch. I took his arm and helped him walk to the kitchen area and sit at the black granite counter. Galena served us before joining us. Her homemade borscht was my father's favorite, and we often had a big bowl for lunch.

Our family adored Galena because she took such good care of our father. She was a redhead with a ready smile who had moved to the U.S. from Siberia, where she had studied engineering. She taught herself English and, at my request, taught me some Russian. I asked her to tell me the worst curse word she knew. I wanted a way to appropriately describe Dad's third wife in a way that my siblings and I could share without anyone else knowing what we were saying. We enjoyed using her new nickname, "Suka," a nasty but apt term for our father's ex-wife.

Galena was good company for Dad. Because she was smart, she could talk with him about his inventive ideas and was always ready to play a game of chess. She responded to my father's increasing mental confusion without making him feel ashamed. She told me that sometimes he would wake her in the middle of the night and ask her to help him exercise. Galena would put on some music, and my father would "dance," which she told me meant he would stand in the kitchen and try to walk to music while holding her hand to steady himself. After a few minutes, he would ask for a snack.

When Dad's routine became laden with many different medications, I went to CVS and bought him individual pill cases, each labeled to avoid mix-ups. On my birthday lunch visit, I watched as Galena placed his pills on the placemat next to his water glass. He took them, and she served him his soup.

"Give me my pills," Dad said.

"You just took them," Galena gently reminded him.

"No, I didn't."

Galena looked at me, and I told my father that he had, indeed, taken them. "No," he yelled. "Give me my pills now!"

I knew Galena didn't want to give him a double dose, but he pushed. My father didn't often get angry, but there was no arguing with him when he did. Galena looked at me helplessly and gave him more pills.

After he died, I learned that the pills he was demanding were steroids. That he had been keeping a secret record of how many he took each day. That he had multiple steroid prescriptions from different doctors. We think he had them filled at different pharmacies to avoid detection. Did my brilliant father believe that the steroids would make him strong? Did he believe they could keep his cancer at bay? Towards the end of his life, when he was fighting so hard to stay alive, I think he did.

"Tomorrow is Randy's birthday." We had finished lunch when Dad announced this. I don't recall what else he said because I was so astonished that he had remembered my brother's birthday and not mine. Our birthdays are one day apart, and for a moment, I thought he was teasing me. But he wasn't. I didn't say anything.

I went back to work. That was my last birthday with my father. He died two months later.

November 8, 2006

The weather was cold and rainy. My father, Leonard Greene, was suffering in the end stages of his five-year battle with lung cancer. He was bundled up, wearing the navy-blue ski hat that he often wore—even during the previous summer—to keep warm. His once tall body now stooped and frail had to be helped into the car's passenger seat. His usual caretaker had been unable to work that day, and a substitute aide stood in the doorway. She didn't understand why my father's attorney had told her to stay in the house and not accompany her charge. She watched as the lawyer drove my 88-year-old father away.

Two hours later, he was driven home.

Three weeks later, he was dead.

Final Days

My father lay in his hospital bed motionless. An oxygen mask covered his nose and mouth. His pale blue eyes were closed.

This was how he was for most of the time that week. I held his hand and squeezed it occasionally to see if there was any response. There wasn't. I can't remember him responding to anything.

I noticed that the top of his hand seemed to be sweating. Not really sweating, but his pores had opened up. I had never seen anything like it—it looked like his hand was crying. I did not ask about it because I was afraid it meant death was imminent.

Dad's doctor came by and motioned Laurie and me into the hall. He said he needed to speak with us privately. I'm not sure who else was there that day, but probably Stevie, and maybe Terry, Doug, and his wife, Carla. My siblings spent many hours with Dad that week, and the days have blurred into one.

I sat on a couch in the small green lounge while the doctor explained that nothing more could be done. He suggested that, if we approved, he would start a morphine drip. "Knowing Leonard as well as I do," he said, "I'm sure he wouldn't want to linger or suffer in the state he is in now."

Silence. Dad would die in a few days, and the morphine would speed up the process. I said I didn't want him to be in any pain. Together, all of Dad's children approved this final step.

I returned to my father's bedside as the drip was administered. Sitting on the chair beside him, holding his hand, I saw the clear fluid slowly enter his arm. Dad had survived previous cancers and heart surgery, but this time was different. Did he know what was happening? Was he scared? The monitor emitted a steady beep, flashing his heartbeat and pulse rate. I stared numbly as I prepared myself to watch my father die.

When I was young, I thought of White Plains Hospital as a happy place because I had been born there. Since the shock of Phyllis's death in the same hospital, the halls held loss and sadness that I relived each time I entered. Now I was back.

I was determined that Dad would not die alone. He didn't like being alone and often encouraged people to join him. "The more, the merrier," he'd say. I didn't risk taking the time to go home to shower or even change my clothes, and we took turns going out to get food.

One night I fell asleep on a cot in his room, but worried that my snoring might bother him, I asked Carla to sleep there instead, and I moved to the couch in the lounge. This vigil became our routine. We discovered a small pizza parlor next to the hospital, where we took short breaks, more for gathering our emotions than for the pies. Our natural camaraderie was a respite.

On the morning of my father's death, Dr. Sadan, his oncologist, came into the room and stood at the foot of the bed. Dad must have heard us mention her name because he opened his eyes for the first time in days and removed his oxygen mask while reaching his arm toward her. His mouth was open, but no sound came out of it.

Dad and Dr. Sadan had formed a close bond during his long battle with lung cancer. I looked at her, expecting her to comfort him, but she didn't say a thing. Instead, she turned briskly and walked out of the room. I couldn't understand why she reacted like that. Dad dropped his arm and closed his eyes and mouth.

A few hours later, he was gone. Laurie and I held his hands until the monitor stopped so he would know he was not alone.

A few years later, I ran into Dr. Sadan in the hospital while I was undergoing outpatient treatment. We hugged "hello," and I asked her if she remembered the day that my father died. "Yes, of course, I do. I ran out of his room because I didn't want you to see me burst into tears."

CHAPTER TEN

Fallout

The Funeral

Our father's aversion to organized religion and cemeteries precluded him from leaving any instructions for burial. His aversion was so extreme that he refused to plant begonias in his garden because he said they reminded him of cemeteries.

My siblings and I arranged to have Dad's memorial service at the Ethical Culture Society in White Plains. The only other time I had been there was in 1965 when Mommy Phyllis died. Dad's service was only a little more personal than hers. Doug and I read eulogies at Dad's. No one did that for Mommy—I don't think any of us would have had the composure after the shock of her sudden death.

Despite our questions, Dad never told us what he'd done with Mommy Phyllis's remains. So, we planned to have his ashes spread by plane over his farm in Montana.

After the service, family and close friends came to our house for Shiva. Our Rabbi led a traditional service, and we all recited the Jewish mourners' prayer. I told Randy I thought Dad would have approved.

Randy disagreed. "I wouldn't be so sure of that," he said.

When I asked him what he meant, he replied, "You'll find out tomorrow." Then he walked out the front door.

An hour later, he sent an email calling for a family meeting the following morning at Safe Flight. He said not to ask him any questions because he wouldn't say more about it. Knowing that I wouldn't sleep, I called my father's attorney and asked him to tell me what was happening.

"The fact is, Bonnie, your father disinherited you."

Seven Prior Wills

Leonard Greene's lawyer, who executed Dad's last Will and Testament and had written seven prior wills during the last year of my father's life, was deposed in August 2007. In the notes from that deposition, I learned that all of those prior wills were signed either at my father's house or at Safe Flight's offices. But on the day his lawyer had my father sign his final will, he brought him somewhere else, somewhere Dad had never been. The notes state that "Leonard Greene's last will was duly signed under the watchful eyes of [his lawyer] and several witnesses who had never met Leonard Greene. They attested that the frail, visibly confused stranger was of sound mind."

The Will

"The fact is, Bonnie: Your father disinherited you."

"Why? What did I do?" I stammered.

The lawyer sighed. "I knew you would think that. You did not do anything. You were all disinherited, Bonnie. He basically left everything to the Institute."

Closing my eyes, I tried to grasp his words. I tried to pretend I didn't hear them. My stomach seized. My first impulse was to call my father and have him straighten out this obvious mistake.

Placing the phone back in its cradle, I sat in the chair for a long time. *What happened?* I asked myself, over and over.

I felt more bewildered than disappointed. Dad had always been a generous provider, while at the same time, he taught us that we needed to be financially responsible and independent. I never expected him to bequeath me fabulous wealth; it wasn't his style. However, I assumed he would leave us each a safety net, perhaps a modest annual income that could help cover unexpected medical expenses or supplement our grandchildren's education. My only consolation was that he had treated us all equally, and so I stopped wondering if I had done anything to incur his anger. Not that he was the vindictive type. I remember him telling me that the one thing he hadn't liked about his father-in-law (my Grandpa Al) was that he used to say to his sons he would disinherit them if they did or didn't do one thing or another. My father never used his wealth to threaten or bribe behavior. I couldn't begin to understand his last act—this final and incomprehensible message to his children.

I had promised the lawyer not to tell anyone about our conversation, and I kept my word. How could I tell my siblings this unbelievable news? I spent a sleepless night waiting for the next day's meeting when they would find out. I unsuccessfully tried to convince myself that this was all a mix-up that would soon be cleared up.

The following day, I joined most of my siblings (Laurie had returned to Montana) at Safe Flight to meet with Dad's attorney. I walked past my father's office and peered through the doorway. Everything looked the same: pale blue carpet, blue and green couch and matching chairs, shelves filled with books, photographs, and aviation memorabilia. I yearned to see him sitting at his large teak desk.

Sliding glass doors led to a small patio with the wrought iron table and chairs he had kept from the house on Whig Road in Scarsdale, where Randy, Laurie, and I had once lived. That was the table where Dad and I would sometimes have lunch on warm days when we were both working at Safe Flight.

Dad's office was where we spent so many hours talking comfortably about anything without the malevolent presence of his third wife. It was what my siblings and I thought of as a Suka-free zone. Even though he never admitted it, I know Dad also considered Safe Flight a place where he could be more relaxed with his children than at his house.

There were less poignant memories in the conference room, where we assembled around the long mahogany table. The lawyer came in and briefly explained the details of the will. Despite telling me the night before that Dad had disinherited all of us, he announced that Dad had left his farm in Montana to Laurie. Laurie and her husband owned the farm adjacent to Dad's, and they had worked that farm for Dad for the past 30 years. I tried to accept that it made sense for her to inherit it.

As for Safe Flight, that was left to Randy to continue to run. Many years before his death, Dad had given each of his children

Safe Flight common stock. When Donny was killed, Randy had become Safe Flight's president, the position Donny was supposed to have taken on his return from New Orleans. Randy alone had 100 percent of the voting stock, and now he also had complete control of the business.

Stunned, we waited for someone to speak. The lawyer stood awkwardly at the doorway and continued: "There is one more bequest in the will."

I was not expecting this. He said that Dad had left all of his children, except Randy, a separate entity that held seven of our father's recent patents. The company was called Greenleaf Innovations. I instantly understood Dad's choice of the name. When his grandfather emigrated from Poland in the 1880s, his name was Greenblatt, meaning "green leaf." In America, he changed his name to Greene, and it touched my heart that my father remembered his heritage in naming the company that he left to his children. I learned that Greenleaf had been formed a year before my father's death and, I later found out, before steroid-induced dementia had overtaken his brilliant mind.

When we asked about the patents, Dad's lawyer said he didn't know much about them. He looked uncomfortable; he was pretty quiet on the subject. In hindsight, that was the day I first noticed his habit of uneasy squirming.

Many of my father's patents were mounted on plaques on the wall behind his desk. Perhaps the seven patents we had inherited in Greenleaf would be valuable and potentially a source of income for me and the other siblings who had been left out of his estate. One might become as successful as the Stall Warning Indicator, which is on permanent display in the Smithsonian National Air and Space Museum. Maybe Dad had, indeed, left us something of value.

My hopes were short-lived. Randy didn't waste any time informing us that the patents legally belonged to Safe Flight and that Dad didn't have the right to leave them to us. Randy added that the Greenleaf patents were not all finalized and that, even if they were, he would not let us have them. "They're probably valueless," he said. (I discovered later that only one of the seven patents had been registered.)

We spent the rest of that long morning trying to get Randy to agree on ways to remedy our situation.

"Would you buy the patents from us?"

"No"

"Pay us royalties if they ever sell?"

"No"

I was astounded. Randy gave us no explanation for his harsh attitude. Did he feel we were less deserving of Dad's estate than he and Laurie were? I was hurt and angry. If he had let us keep the patents, we might not have tried to contest the will.

Then someone noticed that there was no mention of Donny's children in the will, nor were they included in the Greenleaf bequest. My father had adored Donny, and I knew he would never in his right mind have left out Charlie and Jody, who were father-less after 9/11. Almost as strange was the fact that Dad's lawyer, the executor of the will, was one of Donny's closest friends. *Why were they omitted?* I wondered. None of it made any sense.

Our grief-stricken family meeting ended with Randy getting up and threatening to sue Dad's lawyer and all of us for the patents if we did not agree to sign them over to Safe Flight. Then he walked out of the room.

Dad's lawyer followed, but not before turning to tell us we could call him if we wanted. Clearly, he didn't believe that my father had meant to disinherit us. I later discovered that he had told Doug and Steve privately after the memorial service to contest the will. He advised them that the family should sue the estate to distribute our father's holdings more equitably and treat the family as my father had always stated was his intention. He even offered to help us.

I was determined at least to keep the patents that Dad had left us. I couldn't pretend that he had treated us equally, and I couldn't help but ask why.

Lawyers

Despite our differences, Randy and Laurie soon agreed to join us in trying to overturn the will. And we unilaterally decided to include Donny's children in the lawsuit.

A few weeks after our initial meeting at Safe Flight, Randy, Steve, and I drove into Manhattan to interview potential law firms to represent us. Randy's personal lawyer had given him some suggestions, and we met with a few before settling on a prestigious firm that had won many high-profile contests over wills.

Susan, a senior partner, greeted us in the firm's top-floor conference room. I took in the floor-to-ceiling windows framing panoramic views of Manhattan and the enormous mahogany table and leather chairs set with monogrammed pens and legal pads at each place. More lawyers joined Susan for the interview to determine, I assumed if it was worth their trouble to take the case. Dressed in our casual clothes, we didn't look like high-net-worth clients.

We explained to Susan that our father had been extremely ill in the last three months of his life and had demonstrated many incidents of significant confusion. One was that shortly before his death, he drafted a $50,000 half-page ad for the New York Times extolling the virtues of the Institute. In it, he stated that he, Leonard Greene, was the number one enemy of Osama Bin Laden. He went as far as to offer to trade his life for Bin Laden. (Terry saw the draft and convinced him not to submit it.)

At this point, we didn't know that Dad had signed *seven* wills in those last months. We only knew about the final one, which was signed just three weeks before he died. Susan told us it was extremely difficult to overturn a will, but they would look into our case.

Besides the Montana farm and Safe Flight, the bulk of Dad's estate was left to the Institute for Socio-Economic Studies, a nonprofit think tank he founded in the early 1970s to study welfare and healthcare reform.

The Institute had once been politically active. It funded research at Columbia University and held annual dinners with esteemed speakers like Margaret Thatcher and other dignitaries. My father assembled a group of physicians through the Institute to work on healthcare reform. He presented his proposed Fair Share plan, a national tax rebate of $1,000 a month for all Americans, to legislators and politicians. Not traditionally Democratic nor Republican economic thinking, dad was solving a problem. He tried to give a young man a promotion, but the employee declined and quit. He explained that his salary was putting his income above the ceiling to qualify for subsidized housing. Dad's idea was to shift aid so that it was a floor, not a ceiling. No one would be worse off for working more. The funds received from the government would be taxable along with all personal income, and the money, therefore, would be recouped by the government.

Convinced that he had a plan to "end welfare as we know it," my father offered to fly George McGovern up to New Hampshire to register for the 1972 Presidential campaign. I remember meeting my Dad's plane when it landed in White Plains on their return and thinking how exciting it was. Dad told me that he explained the details of his Fair Share plan on the flight, and Senator McGovern responded favorably. Unfortunately, either McGovern didn't quite get it, or people weren't buying it, and some pundits blamed Fair Share for McGovern's loss to Nixon. (Andrew Yang had a similar plan during his unsuccessful bid for the 2020 Presidency. I wondered if he had read my father's book, "The National Tax Rebate," on the subject.)

At the time of his death, my father was the president, director, and sole decision-maker of the Institute. He had left no exit plan for the organization, no leadership appointments—other than to name his lawyer as secretary, thus giving him rights to determine how to spend the now inactive think tank's millions of dollars.

I could see Susan and her associates figuratively rubbing their palms in anticipation of their hefty legal fees. She had cautioned us that proving mental incompetence was difficult, but now she thought it possible in our father's case. We agreed to hire her, and I drove home feeling a little bit hopeful.

Deposition

The will contest required that Dad's lawyer, my siblings, and I be deposed. My deposition brought me back to the firm's elegant conference room. A videographer sat behind the lead attorney at the head of the table with his camera focused on me. He asked my permission to tape the proceedings, and I agreed, promptly forgetting his presence.

I was absorbed in making our case. Instead, I broke into tears as soon as the lawyer spoke. "Do you remember when your father…?" he asked me, and I put my head down on the table and cried. "I remember everything," I said.

My lawyer requested a break and walked me out of the room so I could compose myself. When I returned, the videographer nodded at me. "I'm sorry for your loss," he said. "I know how painful this is for you." The session continued, and I answered in great detail questions about my father's physical and mental deterioration.

I requested and received a written copy of Randy's deposition, which included some shocking revelations. He testified that Dad had told him about Greenleaf more than a year before he died.

At the time, he said he had told Dad that the patents belonged to Safe Flight, and he'd warned Dad that he would sue us for the patents if he left them to us in his will. Bile rose in my throat when reading his words. Bile and rage. How could Randy have said that? My father was extremely sick at the time and must have felt hurt and powerless.

Years later, I learned why Randy had to protect Safe Flight's assets without explaining why. He did the right thing, but I didn't know it then.

Doug, Steve, and I sat in on Dad's lawyer's deposition. We arrived armed with notes and questions for our attorneys to ask, knowing the Lawyer would be forced to tell the truth.

The Lawyer seemed to squirm at the head of the table as we sat opposite his counsel, the videographer filming the proceedings. Dressed in a dark blue suit, white shirt, and no tie, he appeared increasingly uncomfortable as the questioning progressed. Sweat dripped down his forehead as he leaned back in his chair, almost to the point of falling over. Most of his answers began with a humble smile and "I'm only a country lawyer," which made me increasingly enraged. I glared at him but resisted the urge to tip his chair.

The Lawyer claimed to have no explanation for why my father had changed his will seven times in the final four months of his life. He admitted that he didn't ask my father why he made the changes, even though the last few wills were radically different from his prior wills, leaving substantial bequests to all of his children. When asked why he hadn't discussed the matter with his client, his response was, "If I didn't rewrite it, he would have gotten someone else to do it."

I was disgusted to think that the only plausible reason for continuing to rewrite Dad's will was to keep his fees coming. "Family was everything to Leonard," he testified. Then why hadn't he questioned my father's mental status, just weeks before his death and after months of chemo and steroids? To me, it showed incompetence, if not legal malpractice.

Throughout the day, he continued sweating, leaning back in his chair with his hands clasped behind his head, still describing himself as "just a country lawyer." This "country lawyer" had been hired by my father years earlier to represent Safe Flight, the Institute of Socioeconomic Studies, and Corporate Angel Network. He had a reputation as an expert tax specialist, and my father trusted him completely.

The Lawyer, also considered a family friend, joined us on many occasions—most notably for day sails and family gatherings. He and Donny became close, and I often found him sitting in Donny's office at Safe Flight when I went there for lunch. I, too, trusted him. I used to refer to him jokingly as "my new best friend." I confided in him about my cancer diagnosis, which I kept secret during the last year of my father's life because I didn't want to worry him. Did he forget that I might need over $100,000 yearly for treatments? $100,000 a year that we couldn't afford? Did it occur to him, the father of one, that my brothers and sisters had children and grandchildren whom we would want to help pay for college? In the previous wills, we were all left trusts. It was my father's desire to provide for us.

And how could he have forgotten to include Donny's children in the will revisions? When Donny was killed, this supposed best friend was at his house even before I got there, about an hour after I heard the unimaginable news. Donny's children should have been foremost in his mind, yet they weren't even mentioned.

Instead, The Lawyer was appointed executor, allowing him control of many millions of dollars. While the money didn't go to him directly, as director of the Institute, he would handle all the money that my father had left to it.

When The Lawyer was young, his father died, and he always told us that he thought of our dad as a father. I believed him. And I knew Dad was extremely fond of him. I wondered if he saw himself as betraying his mentor, his client, and his friend. The injustice was too much for me to accept, so I focused on the will contest, hoping to overturn it.

It was evident to anyone who spent a few minutes with Dad that he was not acting or thinking clearly during his last months. The critical question was: Why didn't The Lawyer insist on a mental status evaluation before complying with our father's wishes?

By this time, I was not surprised that Dad's lawyer had not told us the truth about Greenleaf when he said he didn't know anything about it. While being deposed, he admitted that he had drafted the legal papers for Greenleaf and had the documents to prove it.

My father asked Laurie several times to reach his lawyer during his last hospitalization. The Lawyer refused to communicate with Dad directly, instead telling her, "It is time for the family to be with him."

When asked why the final will disinherited most of Dad's children, he shrugged his shoulders and said he did not know. Notes from his deposition follow:

"Tell me about the decedent's relationship with his children."

The Lawyer sat back. "Leonard loved his family above all else."

"So, did you ask him why the changes?"

"No"

"Did you consider having a doctor evaluate his mental status?"

"No."

"What did the original will leave his children?"

"About a million dollars each."

Concurrent with the process of contesting the will, the battle over the seven patents continued. For the first time since Dad and Phyllis married, the family divided into two bitter camps: Randy and Laurie versus the rest of us. Randy repeated his threat to sue us if we didn't sign the patents over to Safe Flight.

My resistance to his demands caused a volcanic rift in our relationship, which was additionally challenging for me because he was the chairman of Corporate Angel Network, where I worked. His argument for denying us the rights to the patents was that Dad had "invented" them at Safe Flight. I argued that Safe Flight itself was our father's invention and that he had often "invented" at home or out of the office. His most famous invention, the Stall Warning Indicator, resulted from a fatal air crash he witnessed before Safe Flight was even an entity. Dad did not require a desk or a computer in order to invent. He did not invent from 9 to 5; it was his way of life. I begged Randy to let us keep the ("probably valueless") patents because they were the only things Dad had left us. But Randy stood firm. I wondered, if the patents were useless, why the whole fight over them? Was he lying about their value?

Steve, Doug, and I returned to the law firm and asked them to countersue Safe Flight for the patents. After a few days, the firm's senior partner informed us they couldn't take our case because Randy was a plaintiff in the will contest and a defendant in our suit against Safe Flight. This ended our chances of inheriting the patents. We were back where we began—with no legal representation. I did not know what would come next, but I continued to hope that right would prevail.

One day, I got home from work and found a registered letter demanding that I sign a legal document indicating that I release the patents to Safe Flight. Copies of my sibling's signatures on similar documents told me that I was the last holdout. Finally, beaten down and without the financial resources to pay for more legal fees, I relented. I signed my ownership of Greenleaf over to Safe Flight.

Settlement

Susan's firm agreed to help us with a financial settlement. We had paid the law firm a $25,000 retainer (shared by the seven of us), and I hoped to be reimbursed for some of that. But every service the firm performed added to their bill, and the retainer was quickly spent. Then there were complicated negotiations about the tax implications of the value of the estate—specifically the Montana farm—that I didn't understand.

After almost two years and lots of arguments and ugliness among the siblings, the will was settled. The many months of emails, legal documents, and constant family phone conferences drained much of my physical and emotional energy. When the agreement was signed, we each received enough money to cover the enormous legal fees we had accrued—but not much extra. The settlement dissolved the Institute, with its proceeds split equally among the seven siblings plus Donny's children. These proceeds were legally mandated to be spent on behalf of the Institute for SocioEconomic Studies for any IRS-approved charity—with no benefit to the donor. Had the will not been contested, Dad's lawyer would have had total control of the Institute and its assets. Despite all the iterations of my father's will, The Lawyer had made sure that his role in the Institute didn't change in any of them.

My siblings chose a variety of charities to support with their Institute funds. I chose the New York Community Trust—a donor-approved fund—as the administrator of my portion. I later learned that my father had also donated to them, and I liked the coincidence.

My father often expressed gratitude for the nurses' extraordinary care during his frequent hospitalizations. So, I established the Leonard M. Greene Nursing Scholarship for second-year nursing students who demonstrated financial need. I designated Westchester Community College (where my Dad had been a longtime supporter) to select the recipients and administer the money. I was happy to do this in my father's memory; I would have wanted to do the same thing even if I didn't have the Institute funds to disperse. I knew Dad would have approved. He probably would have said that he was "tickled pink," one of his many favorite expressions, along with "I don't have a dickey bird of an idea," which he said whenever he didn't have an answer to one of my questions. And, of course, "Fooled 'em again!"

Despite my disappointment with the outcome of the will contest, life for the LeVar family went on as usual. My only fear was that we might need funds for healthcare expenses one day, but great wealth had never been a driving force in the way we lived.

My other concern was the rift among my siblings. That took a while to heal, but, finally, it did.

Leonard M. Greene

CHAPTER ELEVEN

Closure

Vlad

A man with a Russian accent answered the phone. "Vlad?" I said.

How could he help me?, he asked.

I said I wanted to talk with him. "To see if anyone wants to contact me."

The year after my father died, I decided to consult a medium. If the dead could communicate with the living, I was eager to hear from my father and Donny. I missed them both so terribly. I wanted to hear that Donny knew that Claudette and his two young children were all right after the shock of his death on 9/11. I wondered if my father knew what had been going on with the will contest the bitter lawsuit, the whole family in emotional turmoil. And then there was my father's missing watch: He had wanted it to go to Doug, and when no one could find it, several of my siblings had asked me if I had taken it. Insulted and hurt by their accusations, I assured them that I did not have the watch. But their allegations continued. For all these reasons, I defied common sense and convention and called Vlad.

Vlad, a medium and psychic healer, had been recommended by a woman whose cancer he had healed. When I dialed his office for an appointment, his assistant informed me that Vlad was in California, but he could do a reading by telephone. I considered how that would work; it seemed like it might be complicated until I reminded myself that connecting with the dead was long-distance, too. I agreed to call him the following week.

I placed the call from my bedroom. Not taking any chances that Vlad could read my mind, I closed the shades and turned all the pictures of my family face down on the dresser. Then I stretched out on the bed in the darkened room and shut my eyes. I tried to concentrate on nothing but our upcoming conversation.

"Tell me your first name, your age, and where you're from," Vlad said, "and if the spirits come, I will stop whatever we are saying and let them interrupt."

Despite any hope I felt, a spiritual "interruption" seemed unlikely. And now I thought of complex star charts and zodiac signs—would answers to only three questions unlock my past? "My name is Bonnie," I said. "I'm 61." And then, without hesitating, I said, "Russia." I didn't know why I said that. I'm a native New Yorker, but my family's country of origin flew out of my mouth. Vlad responded with a chuckle and said that we were from the same place.

Then he said, "You are overweight, your energy is depleted, and I am concerned about your lack of sleep." True, but I wasn't impressed: Many people are overweight and sleep-deprived.

"You also have had breast health problems for the past twenty years." Opening my eyes, I looked around the room for a hidden camera. How did he know that? I supposed that that, too, wasn't unusual for someone my age. Before I had time to think more, Vlad asked, "Who is Betty?"

"Betty? I had a grandmother named Betty. Why?"

"She is here," he answered. I jumped off the bed and started to pace. I had to think for a minute before speaking again. "I had not expected to hear from my grandmother."

"She gave you a necklace," Vlad said. A necklace? Then I remembered the short gold chain with the blue lapis butterfly that she had given me long ago. I loved it; I had worn it for years.

I was feeling a little guilty that I had not included Grandma Betty on my wish list. I had been close with her, and I waited for Vlad to say more, but instead, he paused. "Moishe is here," he said. "Michael." Moishe was my father's Hebrew name. Hearing it jolted me out of my carefully controlled skepticism. I sat down on the bed.

"That's my father!" I gasped. My voice was louder than I expected. Was this another lucky guess, or could Vlad really communicate with the dead? Part of me wanted to hear more, while another part wanted to hang up and call my sisters and brothers to get their reactions.

"Well, your father is here. Who's Max?"

"My grandfather, but he died when my father was very young, and I never met him."

"It doesn't matter. He's here, too." I was curious who else was "with" my father. The idea that my father and grandparents were somehow there with Vlad was both comforting and frightening.

"Who are Rose… and Ida?" Rose was my father's aunt, but I had never heard about an Ida. Maybe Vlad had made a mistake.

Then he announced: "Your father wants to ask you a question. He wants to know, 'How was France?'"

I had gone to France the summer before my father died. I wondered now about the importance of this trip and my grandmother's necklace. I also wondered how my father was "asking" questions.

And there were more—about my sisters, my children, and other family members. I felt foolish talking to my dead father through a stranger on the phone, but at the same time, I didn't want it to end. And I kept hoping that Donny might "show up."

As our session ended, Vlad said, "Your father wants to know who has the watch."

No longer talking through Vlad, I answered my father directly. "I didn't take the damn watch! I don't know where it is!"

Laughing, Vlad explained, "He's making a joke." My father and I knew how to push each other's buttons, and this "joke" pushed mine. First, his Hebrew name, and now the ability to make jokes? I let go of my doubts. Only my father could have known about the watch, and only he would have known that he was making a joke. My father was with me, still with me.

A few years after my reading with Vlad, I found a folder containing old family documents, including a family tree. At the top of the list were my great-grandparents. My great-grandmother's name was Ida.

Billie's Funeral

When my Uncle Bob called to tell me that my mother had died, I debated whether to attend the funeral. Yes, she was the person who had given birth to me. But she was also a stranger who had never made me feel important or a part of her life. And now I knew there could never be a reconciliation.

The strongest emotion she expressed toward me was anger. Anger until the day she died because of the time I ran into her unexpectedly coming out of a restaurant forty years earlier when I was away on a college weekend. She never forgave me for introducing her to my date as "Billie" instead of "my mother."

In hindsight, anything I did would probably have triggered her anger. She maintained a code of anger towards most of the people in her life. Usually, they didn't know its origin. I knew mine and couldn't believe it was enough to permanently write me (and her grandchildren) out of her life.

Now that she was gone, my main concern was respectfully acknowledging her death without compromising my integrity. I decided to "do the right thing" and attend the funeral. Not wanting to go alone, I begged Randy to let me fly up to Boston with him.

Randy was still irritated with me for holding up the settlement when I refused to sign over the Greenleaf patents to Safe Flight. He and Anne didn't say a word to me when we met at the SFIC hangar before the flight. I stepped onto the wing of his blue-and-white, four-seater Beechcraft and sat next to our cousin, Scott, in the back. I hoped that Randy agreeing to fly me to our mother's funeral was a step towards restoring our relationship, but I didn't say anything, afraid that he would change his mind and tell me to get out of the plane.

Billie's house was a well-kept white colonial in a fashionable Boston suburb. I had been there only once over the past 30 years, and as we approached, I remembered a conversation she and I had had then on her back steps. "Some people should never have children," she said. We were talking about someone else, but I knew she included herself in her comment. I wondered how she could look me in the face and admit this. If she hadn't had children, I would never have been born. Rather than assuring me that she wasn't talking about herself, she turned and walked back into the house. I stood there, not knowing what to think. Did my mother really say that I shouldn't have been born?

Now, as we entered a small foyer papered in a green floral design, Randy walked off to find Laurie, and they sat on a couch across the room, talking quietly to each other. I was on my own. I was anxious about meeting the people in my mother's life. Laurie had spent the past months involved with Billie's care; she had traveled to Boston and met with doctors and health care providers. Randy and I had not. Would the mourners in my mother's living room even know that Billie had another daughter and a son?

I would have to introduce myself. My discomfort at identifying myself as "Billie's daughter" heightened as I anticipated disapproval that I had not been at my mother's side during the last years of her life. How could I explain my sudden appearance at her funeral? I decided to say as little as possible.

I found an unoccupied corner, where a few people came over and asked me who I was. When I told them, they said, "It's nice to meet you," or, "I'm glad you came." Apparently, some people knew of my existence, and I wondered what they had heard about me.

Sitting alone, I studied my mother's living room. Everywhere I looked there were pictures and small figurines of dogs. Dogs, dogs, dogs. Especially dachshunds, my mother's favorite. I knew that Billie loved dogs, but nothing had prepared me for such a shrine to these four-legged creatures. I got up to see if there was any evidence that she had children and found one small heart-shaped framed photograph of Randy, Laurie, and me, ages six, four, and one, in the corner of her den. Her three two-legged children. There was also a larger photograph of Laurie that I had taken when I visited her in Montana. I wondered whether Billie would have displayed it had she known I was the photographer. Other than those two pictures, there was no indication of children. A giant bronze dog cookie barricaded the stairway to the second floor with a note taped to it forbidding access, so I never had the opportunity to see if we "existed" upstairs in her room. My Aunt Joan introduced me to Dr. R., a tall, grey-haired man. I extended my hand and introduced myself, and he looked at me with surprise. "I didn't expect to see *you* here!" he said. When I asked him why he said he had heard that I "wasn't a big fan of Billie."

Who was this person? I asked him to explain, and he said he was Billie's therapist, and he knew all about me. Shaking, I rushed back to the den and grabbed the small picture of the three of us. Practically shoving it under his nose, I said, "Look at this picture. This was the last time we lived together. *We did not abandon her.*"

Without taking a breath, he looked at me harshly and said, "There are two sides to every story."

I had promised myself before arriving that I would not make a scene, so I left the doctor's side without telling him to drop dead.

Returning to my seat in the corner, I waited for the memorial service to begin. It consisted of a short statement from Uncle Bob about how much Billie loved music and Camp Lenore. I waited for him to mention her three children, sitting right there in the living room, but his remarks ended with Billie at age 14.

Next came Dr. R., who began by saying that he had seen Billie three times a week as her psychiatrist for the past eighteen years. He described her relationship issues—not in great detail—and I clenched my fists until I felt my nails dig into my palms. I spoke quietly to the woman beside me. She told me she was a nurse who had cared for Billie and was as surprised as I was to hear Dr. R. betray his patient's confidences.

Before we headed back to New York, someone mentioned that Billie's last wish was to be cremated and interred at the grave of her beloved dachshund. I assumed some laws would prevent this from happening, but I was wrong. My mother is buried in a pet cemetery.

She left the bulk of her estate to Riggs Hospital and the remainder to her housekeeper.

Shanksville, 10 Years Later

The weekend I had both dreaded and looked forward to finally arrived. As John, Jonathan, Joanie, and I drove south through New York and New Jersey, the morning sky darkened with rain-threatening clouds. Truck stops and fast food exits slowly disappeared, and the countryside turned into fertile farmland. The spring green of the hills seemed out of place on this September morning, and I assumed their emerald shade resulted from the heavy rains this part of the country had experienced over the summer.

Passing through eastern Pennsylvania, I admired the beauty of the farms. Rolling fields were dotted with pristine red barns whose fenced-in acres were occupied by cows and horses enjoying the morning. The two-lane highway stretched ahead with little traffic as we passed silos, cornfields, and sheets that fluttered in the breeze on clotheslines strung on poles behind back doors. John and I talked about the long weekend's schedule. I looked forward to seeing the other members of our family who would be joining us. Claudette, Charlie, and Jody drove from Connecticut; Stevie and Truddi from Vermont; Terry, Beth, and their son, Ari, from Boston.

Soon we reached the dark green Allegheny Mountains. Snaking around and through them, we arrived at our destination: Shanksville.

About a dozen black motorcycles adorned with American flags were parked at the entrance to our hotel. Wondering what kind of motorcade this was, I learned that the family of Louis Knacke had ridden them thousands of miles from their homes in California. A small group was gathered in the flagged-draped lobby – tired yet enthusiastic about completing their long ride.

Louis Knacke's enormous family attended the memorial services every year. I was looking forward to seeing the other families who would also share this sad anniversary with us. I had become friends with Elsa Strong and her mother during the first-anniversary service. Elsa's sister's name, Linda Gronlund, was alphabetically next to Donny's, and we imagined they had seats in the same row on the plane. It somehow brought us closer. And there was the family of LeRoy Homer, the First Officer of Flight 93. The support and camaraderie of these family members were something I craved. 9/11 and the passing of years without Donny were realities I didn't want to face alone.

Forty passengers had entered that plane. They were strangers, but their families are now our families. We greet one another like long-lost cousins, and each time there is a memorial, we take up where we left off. We remember our loved ones and comfort one another. And we laugh, too.

The events planned for Friday were limited to family members. As we turned onto the winding road leading to the Memorial, I braced myself for the emotions I knew was always close to the surface. I had been to the crash site before, but this visit would be different. This would be the first time we would see the Memorial, which had been completed that year.

No longer could I rummage through the field covered with brush looking for pieces of the plane. When I was here for the third anniversary, I had walked around the site thinking, "Let me find something recognizable, so I will believe that this happened." The year before, Claudette had found a piece of carpet with the United logo—in perfect condition. I was determined to discover some evidence as well.

And I did. I found some twisted green and white electrical wires sticking out of a pile of wood chips. Nearby, I saw a shiny jade-green three-inch-long piece of computer board. The solder, now a decorative squiggle, had once played a part in keeping the plane airborne. When I'd visited my father at Safe Flight, I had often watched as computer boards were assembled, and I never thought I'd see one that had broken apart from a plane because of a terrorist attack.

Donny had worked in the family business, creating safety instruments for airplanes, and the irony of that was not lost on us. Corporate Angel Network, where I worked, was across the street from Safe Flight, and I would often walk over to have lunch with Donny and my father. Donny and I would wander around the area after lunch if the weather was nice. We would sit in his office and chat if the weather wasn't nice. I don't remember many times when he didn't open his desk drawer and proudly showed me his most recent pictures of Charlie and Jody.

I took the piece of computer board, its part number still visible. I thought about giving it to the FBI for further investigation, but I hid it in my pocket instead.

Separated from a magnificent wildflower field by a gently sloped wall, a long stone path led to the Memorial. There, I stood before the Memorial's Wall of Names. Following the line of the flight path, the Wall contained forty vertical slabs of natural white marble, highlighted with patterns of light gray veins. Each slab was unique. Each bore the name of an individual who had perished on September 11, 2001, on United Flight 93.

I walked along the Wall, reading the names of people I had never met yet will never forget. Then I stood by my brother's name, "Donald Freeman Greene." I traced my finger along the letters knowing he was not buried there but thinking this is as close as I was going to get. It was still hard to believe, even inscribed in marble.

We followed the Wall to a heavy wooden gate, through which we entered the field of wildflowers and the crash site. Many of us had been here before, and we were relieved to see that it looked the same. The first responders and all those involved with the investigation and recovery of the remains had been careful to keep the area as intact as possible. The trees, scorched by the plane's crash, still stood as guardians. They had grown, and there were more wildflowers. And now, there was a 17-ton boulder marking the point of impact.

As we walked through the muddy field, I had time to be alone with my thoughts. Other family members appeared to be doing the same. A gentle rain added to the already saturated land, and the mud was up to our ankles. Some people took off their shoes and walked barefoot through the muck; others plodded on, circling the boulder, placing flowers, notes, and small items of remembrance on it, or just touching it. This was where, on Monday, the unidentified remains of the passengers and crew of United Flight 93 would be buried together in three caskets because it was impossible to identify individual remains.

Vice President and Dr. Biden; President Clinton; President George and Laura Bush; Speaker of the House, John Boehner; and the Secretary of the Interior, Ken Salazar, walked slowly past the marble slabs on their way to the podium set beside the marble wall. As I sat in the cordoned-off area reserved for family, my throat tightened with the effort to control my tears. These people were coming to honor my brother and the other passengers and crew of Flight 93. They flew or drove to this remote area in Pennsylvania to spend their day with us. Thousands of private citizens, many waving American flags, stood on the hills behind us. They, too, wanted to honor our family members.

President Bush spoke of their sacrifice: "At the moment America's democracy was under attack, our citizens defied their captors by holding a vote… The most likely target of the hijacked plane was the United States Capitol… Our nation will be forever grateful." As he returned to his seat, he recognized Stevie from prior meetings and smiled warmly at him.

Next came President Clinton, who was having a tough time not choking up. "They saved the terrorists from claiming the symbolic victory of smashing the center of American government," he said of the passengers and crew.

Vice President Biden, a man who has experienced great personal sorrow, looked at us with sincerity and said: "I know what it's like to receive that call... And I know that this is a bittersweet moment for you... their names are going to be etched forever into American history."

After the ceremony, we gathered with the speakers to talk privately. When I was speaking with President Clinton, I realized that I was holding the canvas bag I'd gotten at the Clinton Presidential Library. I told him how much I'd enjoyed the Library, and then I said to him that I'd lived around the corner from his Chappaqua house. In response, he squeezed my shoulder.

Sunday dawned clear and sunny. We had to get to the Memorial early to pass extensive security checks. With no appetite for breakfast, I took an apple from the hotel to eat later.

As our car climbed over the ridge approaching the Memorial, I looked down into the valley and saw dozens of film trucks, each attached to a satellite disk. Surrounding the parking area and the access road to the entrance were state troopers and local police cars. The sight of the media, security, and thousands of people standing behind security fences, all hoping to watch the ceremony, reminded me that this was a public event. All those people would witness our private grief because they cared. They cared about the events of 9/11 and wanted to pay tribute to "The Heroes of Flight 93."

The slowdown at the security check irritated me. When the TSA officer examined my pocketbook, he said I could not take my apple with me. I lost my temper and reminded him he was there because terrorists had killed my brother. I then held out my picture of Donny for him to see. He said he had to speak with his supervisor about the apple, and I stood there and took a bite of it. He returned and explained that it could be used as a missile. I held up the line defiantly as I continued to eat the apple.

Entering the seating area for family and guests, I calmed down. I noticed that police on large mahogany horses were mounted alongside the TV trucks. Several helicopters hovered around the field's perimeter so that no one would know which one carried the president. Finally, we heard one land behind the trees, and President and Mrs. Obama entered the site from behind the Memorial Wall. Dressed in black, they walked hand in hand with their heads bowed toward the seating area.

President and Mrs. Obama standing at the Wall of Remembrance.

They stopped at the floral wreath the Honor Guard had placed in front of the Wall of Names. It sat right in front of Donny's name. I imagined President Obama silently reading it. It made me proud.

Following the public ceremony, family members had private time with the Obamas. I stood next to a teenager who, like many family members, wore a pin with a picture of his mother. When Mrs. Obama greeted him, he uttered, "You look like my mother." She looked at his pin, then at him, and, hugging him, replied, "Yes, I do." That was my moment to shed some tears.

After the president's departure, we witnessed the dedication of the Flight 93 National Memorial, which had just been completed. Governor Tom Ridge and former Governor Tom Corbett spoke. Corbett said, "They engaged in that battle armed only with the knowledge that they were right." As in other years, family members recited the names of the 40 Heroes while a bell tolled for each one.

I had difficulty sleeping Sunday night, knowing that the next day we would participate in a private burial ceremony of the unidentified remains of the passengers and crew of United Flight 93.

On Monday, we gathered at the site. A multi-denominational service was held to honor each passenger's religion. We all placed long-stemmed red roses on each of the three caskets. The only visible marker of the grave would be the boulder. Its great weight and immovability seemed appropriate.

Moving Day

Even standing on a stepladder, I had to stretch to reach the top shelf of the kitchen cabinet in Claudette's house. I was helping her pack up the home where she and Donny had lived with Charlie and Jody. Now, eleven years after his death, the family was moving to a neighboring town.

I felt around in the back corners, hidden from sight, to see if everything had been removed. Suddenly my fingers touched the stem of a small glass. As I pulled it into view, I heard Claudette whisper from behind me: "Careful."

Cradled in a glass that resembled a small brandy snifter, a hand-painted egg rested on a nest-like cushion of straw-colored shredded paper. Practically weightless, the egg was decorated with tiny pale blue stars on a plum-toned background. It was hollow, its insides removed without breaking the shell. Inscribed around it in small white letters was a passage I recognized from "The Little Prince:" *"If you love a flower that lives on a star, it is sweet to look at the sky at night. All the stars are a-blossom with flowers."*

I knew instinctively that I was holding something extraordinary relating to 9/11. The determination to craft such a precious and unique object must have been the work of someone who understood the enormity of the loss. "A friend from Japan made this for me when Donny was killed," Claudette said.

Donny. My brother. The one person in our family who could be counted on to give and receive love and kindness with a joy for life. Taken from our lives abruptly, violently, and permanently.

Not for a minute had Donny been far from my mind that day. We wrapped up a blue and yellow chipped clay mug that Charlie had made as a young boy and Jody's crayoned school papers marked with a teacher's A+. We sorted and labeled containers of photos: Donny and Claudette smiling in front of a ski lodge, Donny at the helm of a small sailboat, Charlie and Jody playing on a beach. The accumulation of a family's life filled box after box.

We spent that hot and humid day carrying memories to the new house. Each time I drove up the driveway for another carload, I recalled Donny's delight whenever company arrived. There, we celebrated many family birthdays and Christmas and Thanksgiving dinners, where we enjoyed barbeques and just sat around in the family room year after year, watching the cousins grow.

The new house, smaller by necessity and design, was only a few miles from the old one. I took the fragile egg, layered it in bubble wrap, and held it in my lap for the short drive. I brought it inside and stood still for a moment, gazing at it. Then, Claudette and I gently placed it on the corner shelf above the sink in her new kitchen.

Donny, Claudette, Jody, and Charlie – Winter 2000

Camelot Revisited

Sometimes I go out of my way to drive past the two-hundred-year-old white colonial on Bedford Road so I can glance over at the multi-paned windows on the second floor where my bedroom once was. I can picture the pale blue wallpaper sprinkled with daisies that Phyllis let 11-year-old me choose before we moved into what would become my happiest childhood home.

The road can get busy, so driving by doesn't give me much time to look at the beautiful old house. But I can see that there is now a stone wall in front where a white wooden fence with black trim once stood. And there is a wrought iron gate at either end of the semi-circular driveway where none had been. Still, the house looks remarkably the same as it did when we lived there. I check my rearview mirror to see if there is enough distance between me and any traffic behind me to slow down and take in the large side yard where my brothers, sisters, and I played running bases in the rain. I spot the sloping backyard and remember Dad's "specimen" trees, the barn, and the riding rink. In the spring, if there are no cars behind me, I brake for a few seconds to admire the massive magnolia tree standing between the carport and the kitchen door, still blooming after all these years. How I loved those pink blossoms that would blanket our driveway.

Occasionally my father kept Safe Flight's green-and-white pickup truck in the carport—now a closed garage. Once he asked me to return it to Safe Flight, but I told him I was afraid because I had never driven a truck. He insisted, so I said, "Okay." I turned the key, but it wouldn't start. Relieved, I went back into the house and phoned him to explain that I couldn't drive it. I doubt he believed me, but he sent someone from the office to see what was wrong. The man checked under the hood and discovered that the battery was missing! As pleased as I was that I didn't have to drive, I was nervous knowing that a stranger had stolen a heavy battery from the truck when it was parked on our driveway.

One day, I saw the house listed for sale in the real estate section of our paper. I had not been inside since my father sold it 25 years earlier, and I yearned to see it again. I called my friend Helene, a real estate agent, and asked if she would take me there. I promised her that I would pretend to be a prospective buyer and not say anything to reveal my true motivation. I dressed in what I thought was an outfit befitting a wealthy buyer and tried to look serious.

The owner, a young woman, greeted us at the door and welcomed us into the foyer. I didn't get more than a few steps inside when she said, "You used to live here, didn't you?" What had I done in less than a minute for her to ask that?

I couldn't lie. Yes, I admitted, I had, indeed, once lived there. I expected her to ask us to leave immediately, but instead, she smiled and told me she was used to "visits" from my family members.

"What do you mean?" I asked.

She explained that my father used to visit regularly, as well as my brother Steve, who drove down from Vermont. And there were others, but she couldn't remember their names. I was astonished. Why hadn't they told me about their visits? Would I tell them about mine?

She invited me to look around, and, excusing myself from Helene, I walked through the house, trying to absorb the memories without taking too much of the new homeowner's time. I climbed up the winding staircase to the second floor and peered into what had been Terry's room. I could envision her bassinet against the wall, where I liked to watch her splashing in her tiny bath, and the blue rocking chair by the window where Phyllis held her.

Stevie's room was across the hall. Discouraging entry, his pet monkey, "Junior," resided in a large cage -which was usually open! I would often see Junior sitting on top of Stevie's head, picking through his curly brown hair. If you came too close, Junior would try to urinate on you. Its residency in our house ended when it succeeded in reaching Gaga!

Next came Donny's room, which was between Stevie's and mine. Donny saved all his comic books under his bed, and I would go in there to read them. His wallpaper was an enormous map of the world, and each time the name of an African country changed, he corrected it with an indelible marker. By the time Africa became divided up the way it is today, the wall was an inky mess.

My room, once covered with the blue daisy wallpaper that Mommy let me pick out, held too many memories for me to linger there.

Laurie's room was adjacent to mine, in the corner. We spent time sitting on her bed telling secrets, playing games, and trying to escape the shenanigans our brothers liked to pull whenever Dad and Phyllis went out.

Across the hall from my room was our parents' bedroom. It had a large picture window facing the back, and the view was spectacular: seven acres of rolling lawns and many trees. I usually ran up to their room after school, eager to tell Phyllis whatever was on my mind. There she would be, sitting in a swivel chair by the window, sometimes reading, but mostly just waiting for us to come home from school. That was our time with her.

I continued up to the third floor, where Chucky, Randy, and Doug each had rooms. Chuck's room was directly above mine. He had a boa constrictor that escaped from time to time, so I didn't spend much time there. Randy's room was next to Chucky's, and I didn't spend much time there either. Doug had the largest room, but he was often out with his friends.

Returning downstairs, I entered the kitchen. It was modern, with skylights and the latest appliances. Gone was the old gas stove where Lillie had made so many delicious meals. I felt like the heart of the house had been ripped out.

I quickly headed down the three steps to the "gym." This had been the center of our indoor activities, with a half-length basketball court, a trampoline, and a jukebox filled with all the popular records (no nickels needed!). I spent hours playing the jukebox while jumping on the trampoline. All that remained now was the basketball court; the jukebox and the trampoline were gone.

I wished I could stay longer, but I knew we should leave. As we strolled outside, the owner asked if I was the daughter who had gotten married in the backyard.

"Yes," I replied, surprised that my father had told her about my wedding. She said he had described to her how beautiful it was. I felt enormous joy. I wished that he were still alive to talk to about our secret visits to this house, to share the different memories it conjured.

As Helene and I drove out the driveway for what I knew would be the last time, I was comforted by the knowledge that I was not alone in considering this home to have once been our Camelot.

"The End of the World"

The plane banks over the mountains as we approach the Kalispell airport while Terry and I sit across from each other, playing cribbage. The clear, sunny day allows us to see Laurie's farm in the valley below. We will be landing in a few minutes, and

I am looking forward to our sisters' weekend in Montana. Randy will stay with us for a short visit, then fly on to the West Coast and return on Sunday to pick us up.

"Pull up! Pull up!" A recorded voice from the cockpit breaks through the quiet cabin. "Pull up! Pull up!" Terry and I look at each other – and at the rapidly approaching mountains – so close that we can see the individual trees. "The cockpit door is open – as it usually is – and I don't hear anything from Randy or his co-pilot. "This is it," I think. Then the plane makes a steep ascent, banks again, and Randy executes a gentle landing. "What was that?" I ask.

"Oh, we were testing a new instrument," Randy replies, not at all aware that Terry and I had been expecting imminent death. I remember my long-ago flight with Dad, when he neglected to tell me he would be taking a short nap before a difficult landing. Like father, like son. "Fooled 'em again!" I think.

Randy, Laurie, Terry & I in Kalispell, MT. This was taken when we landed that day. It was our last picture together.

Aviation has played a significant role in my life. Safe Flight, of course. All those flights in Dad's King Air, to Vermont, Bermuda, Canada, and Florida. Sleeping in hammocks in the DC-3 as we traveled across the country to go to Disneyland. Dad and Randy, both skilled pilots, were inducted into the Society of Experimental Test Pilots – an honor mainly held by astronauts. But I never felt entirely safe flying until Donny was killed. Of all my fears – wings falling off, running out of fuel, lightning hitting the plane, being hijacked to Cuba – I never imagined terrorists using airliners as missiles. Since 9/11, I have stopped predicting disasters, and I fly without fear.

On Sunday, Randy picks us up in Kalispell as scheduled. About an hour out of White Plains, he says, "Come quickly and look at this!" Terry and I stick our heads into the small cockpit and peer out the window. Randy is pointing toward the horizon line ahead. Above the line, the sky is dark blue. Below the line, it is daylight. No sun or moon is visible. "It's very rare to be able to see this," Randy tells us.

"What am I looking at?" I ask.

"It's the division between day and night," he explains. "You can see the end of the world from here."

The image slowly softens and disappears as we fly home.

Home

Now, there are three homes. Besides mine and John's, there are the homes of our children and their children, our grandchildren. Being with them carries forward the happiness I felt growing up in a large, new family with two loving parents.

Joanie and Bobby are in the town next to ours, so we see them often. Jonathan and his wife, Heather, are in New Jersey, an hour's drive away if there's no bridge traffic. The joy of visiting our grandchildren without needing a plane ticket is something I do not take for granted.

The birth of Sarah, our eldest, was exciting from the first — starting with my misadventures driving to the hospital. As soon as Jonathan called to say that Heather was in labor, I grabbed my coat and ran out of work. Not knowing how to get to the hospital, I assumed there would be signs (none). I asked a policeman (he gave me directions to the wrong hospital). I followed an ambulance for a short while, hoping it would lead me there (no). Finally found a Weight Watchers meeting where someone knew the way. Despite the detours, I made it in time to wait for Sarah's arrival

Next came Matthew, Sarah's brother. John and I were the appointed babysitters for Sarah while Heather and Jonathan were at the hospital. When Sarah woke up the morning Matthew was born, she came into her parent's bedroom, saw us in their bed, and, before I could explain anything, exclaimed, "Mommy's at work!"

Charlotte, Joanie and Bobby's first child, took her time being born. The waiting drove me so crazy, that I finally called the delivery room—only to find out that Charlotte had been born an hour earlier and her parents wanted some time alone with her first.

Samantha was next. Three-year-old Charlotte was in love with her baby sister from the first moment she saw her in Joanie's hospital room. When a nurse came in to fetch Samantha for some post-delivery procedures, Charlotte cried, "NO! Don't take my baby sister away!"

They say grandchildren are the reward for putting up with one's teenage children. Let's just say we love ours a lot!

Epilogue

Randy and I continued to meet for lunches and left the will contest behind. I burst into tears the day Randy told me he was selling his house and moving out of state. He would be the last of my siblings to leave, and my feelings of loss and abandonment resurfaced. I was surprised by how sad I was, and I made him promise to come back often. I silently hoped that Safe Flight would need his attendance regularly.

The last time I walked across the street from CAN for lunch with Randy at Safe Flight, I walked through the building and chatted with some of the employees who had worked there for years, several of whom had been around back when I worked there. Safe Flight is a company where employees are in no hurry to retire.

As I entered the cafeteria, where my father had been offering free lunches for 60 years, it hit me: Randy was my last connection to Dad and Safe Flight, and when he left, he would take that connection with him. I was mourning the loss of Safe Flight and the loss of the refuge I always could find there—the loss of that sense of belonging.

Randy moved to Colorado in December 2020. He called me to tell me he had ALS (Lou Gehrig's Disease) in January. He died the following September, two weeks after our birthdays.

One afternoon, while crossing a busy street with my grand-children, the chirping sounds of the walk sign startled me. Here was yet another of my father's inventions, designed to alert the blind when it was safe to cross the street. Smiling, I thought about the millions of people who have benefited from my father's contributions and his brilliant mind. I whispered a silent, "Thank you, Dad."

Matthew, Charlotte and Samantha

Samantha, Charlotte and Sarah